Desperate Dogs
Determined Measures

Helping shelters save more lives.

ISBN #: 978-0-9857413-0-3

You can't save all the animals in the world...

but you can save one...

join the revolution!

Please log onto www.boundangels.org
and learn more about our work

Chapters

Introduction

Everyone's participation is important in shaping the behavior of difficult dogs. Skilled handlers are essential, but those who support their work and help reinforce the training also help save lives. Putting aside ego is the most important step. There is more than one way to get to a destination and there is more than one way to train a dog. The old saying is funny, but often true:

The only thing two dog trainers can agree on is that the third trainer is wrong.

This often holds true among unskilled trainers. Competent trainers share ideas and work together in order to arrive at the common goal: a solid working relationship between man and dog. Since training is often more art than science, differences abound. In this book, I will share several techniques and hope that you will use any approach in order to help those who need our help. I hope you will choose compassion over ego and that you will look at the world through the eyes of the dog you are trying to help. Because dogs can't talk, no one may be able to tell if you are being compassionate, but you will know in your heart. The dog you are helping knows, and he will never betray you – even if you abuse and betray him. It is a huge responsibility – please take it with compassion and kindness.

Here are some core competencies of dog training expertise:

Level 1– Once completed, a student should be able to:

- Work neutral dogs on basic training, obedience and engagement.
- Maintain a dog's attention.
- Use basic commands such as "sit" and "down".
- Walk a dog on a loose leash.
- Use food or toys to engage dogs.

Level 2 – Once completed, a student should be able to:

- Work with a withdrawn dog on basic interaction.
- Bring withdrawn dogs to a calm place and do basic dog-to-dog introductions in neutral situations. This includes friendly dogs and shy dogs.
- Handle mid-drive dogs.

Level 3 – Once completed, a student should be able to:

- Gain focus of higher-drive dogs.
- Cap a dog's drive and engage higher-drive dogs to channel their energy into excited obedience.
- Give corrections to dogs for sloppy play and for not minding.
- Redirect unfocused energy to productive training or interaction.

**Level 4** – Once completed, students should be able to:

- Clearly understand a dog's drive.
- Understand how to block aggressive behaviors.
- Redirect aggression into focus toward the handler.
- Read a dog's drive and correct him from aggression to focus or neutrality.
- Handle dog-to-dog introductions, correct aggressive behavior and render an aggressive dog neutral to another dog.

To be a competent dog handler/trainer you must strive to work with dogs of all temperaments, breeds, sizes and life-stages. In order to do this properly, it is important to forgo the limits set by any "method" of training or any "style" of training. To work with dogs, it is critical to take into consideration their instincts and their individuality: _what works for one dog may not always work for another dog_. When one system fails, is it fair to throw away all hope for the dog you are working with, or is it worthwhile to step outside the _box of reason_ and see if another method might work? In order to save dogs and transform their lives, we need to be open to any option necessary. We need to be fair and understand that all dogs are not created equally. We need to put aside any preconceptions and stereotypes cast upon us and these dogs. We must strive to save these creatures by any means necessary.

Before you begin reading, please understand that this book is a guide created for shelters and rescue organizations to better understand the difficult behaviors dogs exhibit while living in the stressful environment of the shelter. These tools, lessons and guidance are offered to give a chance to those dogs that are often (and almost immediately) written off for bad and destroyed.

For those shelters that have the luxury of comprehensive behavior modification programs, many of these tools will serve only to evaluate which dogs should be placed into the programs and give some guidance to the best options available for them. To the remaining shelters that struggle with the time and financial constraints that plague our nations shelters, these tools should give a snapshot into the dog's inner personality, provide a better understanding of his issues, and hopefully show that many more can be saved. It is through confusion and misunderstanding that shelter staff and volunteers often have to make the painful decision to destroy dogs that could otherwise be saved. Using the techniques in this book I hope you will be able to save those lives that otherwise would be lost.

The lessons contained in this book are not the only way to train, nor are they recommended to the average pet owner. They are geared to work with the shelter dogs that desperately need the extra attention, care and guidance to save their lives and give them a chance at a loving forever home. Although some of the lessons may seem rough or abrupt, I feel they are not as abrupt as forcing dogs to linger l in the shelter environment or be killed because no one stepped up to show them that there is hope through compliance and understanding. Everything contained in this book is geared toward one goal –SAVING LIVES. For the hundreds of dogs that I have worked with, these techniques have saved their lives. To the thousands I was unable to help because of time and logistical limitations, I am sorry. I hope that in a small part this book will help others to learn and understand these tools and thereby spread the knowledge to those who want to help and save more lives.

Nothing in this book is designed as an attack onto a dog; none of these techniques should be used in anger or frustration, but rather with compassion. If we need to stop a dog's dangerous behavior, it should be our goal to do so in order to save his life. If he is in the throes of fear, aggression or frustration, it is our duty to be the voice of reason in order to save his life.

A note on the gender issue: You will see that throughout this book I refer to dogs in the masculine term of he or him. I am aware that dogs have two sexes, but for the sake of consistency, I have used the masculine term to avoid confusion. This is in no way meant to slight the female gender.

I would like to thank so many people who have helped me along the way of rescue: those who have taught me, those who have learned from me, those who challenged me and all of the people that are working toward the same goals. I am grateful that my life has brought me to this place of endless pain and constant reward. My life has been forever changed because of the lives that have touched me and the lives that I have touched. Knowing that my work has made even the slightest difference to creatures that would have otherwise be forgotten gives me the greatest joy.

Thank you to Michael for your help in getting this book to the place where it is. Thank you to Cindy for your constant support and love and being there. When I feel the world is crumbling, you so beautifully show me that the pieces can be put back together again. Thank you Ed for being there to test these programs and proving that they do work. And thank you to every person who cares enough to try something – anything before making the most painful decision... for giving a last chance which is what this book is all about. And thank you to the dogs who have touched my life, be they my personal companions or those that have passed through my life through my work. I am a better person for having known all of you!

Robert Cabral

Malibu, 2012

Understanding Dogs

Dogs have co-evolved with humans over thousands of years. History shows that man began associating with the wolf and through years of co-evolution this *domesticated wolf* became what we now know as the *pet dog*. It was a relationship based on usefulness for both parties and the bond has grown stronger over the evolution process. Some believe that man would not have been able to evolve as progressively had it not been for our *four-legged friends.* Although, for the most part, we have grown beyond the practical usefulness of our relationship, the bond has taken on a new level, one that is incomparable in any other cross-species relationship.

The wolf – being a skilled hunter – was useful to assist early man in the hunt, and would derive benefits from the cohabitation, including food, shelter and companionship. Needless to say, humans enjoyed this companionship initially and we continue to enjoy it today – even when we rarely need the dog for help in any working capacity.

Working dogs are an exception. They can be very diverse and provide physical services for handicapped people, emotional support, protection, hunting, and dog sports – including Schutzhund, agility, obedience, fly ball and so much more.

So, as much as we don't currently *rely* on the dog for those initial services that began our relationship, we still enjoy the companionship and camaraderie that our dogs provide. For many people, the dog is a true and trusted companion that enjoys sharing time and emotional companionship with them. Owning dogs has been shown to reduce stress, increase physical fitness and increase lifespan, as well as being a lot of fun. Overall it is a win-win. Dogs live much longer and better quality lives when kept as pets than they could ever hope for in the wild, unless we consider those that are victimized by people who have no compassion. And humans enjoy a better lifestyle when they share their lives with dogs.

Even though we have lived with dogs for all of these years, many still don't seem to understand dogs at their core. Or, I should say that people understand what they want to understand and leave the rest up to fate. This can easily be seen in people's frustrations with their dogs when it comes to training and interacting with a dog they cannot control.

Most people feel that a dog should act as the human wishes, without much work or teaching from the human. Placing this *unfair* expectation onto a dog is often the cause of frustration for people and the reason that dogs end up abandoned at shelters. To clearly understand how a dog thinks, we must strip away that which causes the most frustration between man and canine – speech.

Dogs lack the ability to communicate through speech, and most humans lack the ability to communicate without it. Humans *SAY* what they want the dog to do – the dog doesn't understand what the human is *SAYING* and therefore does something completely different. If we don't teach the dog in a fair manner what a particular word means, it has no meaning to the dog.

Before we begin teaching the dog any system of communication, we should first understand how a dog functions. A dog has two basic drives: *pain* and *pleasure*. His desire is based around his instinctive drive for survival. Everything that brings him pleasure revolves around his desire to survive (i.e., food, shelter, play). Everything that brings him pain revolves around his instinct of self-preservation (i.e., avoiding death, punishment, injury).

Research has shown that humans are the only creatures who understand that they will die. Although other animals may mourn the loss of a partner, they are not aware that eventually the same fate will befall them. When my older dog was sick and dying, my younger dog *could* possibly comprehend that his best friend might eventually "go away"; however, he was not aware that he will eventually travel down that same road.

Even though the dog does not "know" that he will die, he does instinctively know that he needs to do certain things to survive. By understanding these basic *drives*, we are able to clearly shape a dog's behavior into something we can *enjoy living with*. If we understand that a dog "likes" treats, we can manipulate the dog into sitting, standing, lying down or following, by the use of these treats. If we understand that a dog likes to play, we can use the lure of playing, to get him to perform.

Dogs are basically very simple creatures and easy to understand. In fact, they are so simple to understand that it is often our "overthinking" of the dog's mind that causes us the most frustration in trying to "figure out" why the dog is acting like he is. Overthinking our dogs frustrates us almost as much as it frustrates them – and yes, dogs get frustrated.

Imagine meeting someone on a street who doesn't speak your language, and the more he speaks to you, the more frustrated he gets – until finally he is screaming at you. The words may be the same at all volume levels, and yet you still don't understand what it they mean. The person screaming is frustrated and so are you. *So it is for our dogs.* We say something, and then say it again. Then we begin to yell and the message still doesn't get through. The dog will get frustrated and either ignore you or begin shutting down. Neither of these options is good for building a relationship or training.

We need to understand how to clearly communicate with a dog if we want him to do what we want. We also need to understand that what we are trying to get the dog to do must bring *him* pleasure; this can be in the form of praise, food or play – or best yet, a combination of the above.

Learning to understand what the dog is "thinking" is the first step in solving problems, whether they are behavioral or physical. The key to understanding is to lose our preconceptions and our egos. It involves being quiet – something that is very hard for humans to do. When the noise stops, we open the path to communication, be it with dogs or people.

One of the most important aspects to understanding dogs is contained in the chapter ***The Binary Dog***. This concept alone is worth the time you are taking to read this book.

Why Dogs End Up in Shelters

If we can begin to understand dog, we can get a clearer picture of why dogs end up in shelters. Simply put, people place far too many expectations onto their dogs. They see a mental picture of the dog lounging peacefully on the couch, listening to every command the human gives, getting along with everyone and all other dogs (cats too, of course). They see a picturesque walk along the sidewalks of their neighborhood with their faithful companion at their side. The dog only needs to walk when the human decides and, until then, he sits quietly in the house entertaining himself –watching TV, or playing alone and quietly in the yard. When the human decides, the dog will be ready to spring up and play a quick game of fetch, then go back to his role as the *unobtrusive dog*. The ideal picture we paint of the dog is not of a dog, but rather a robot.

Since this is not the situation with most dogs (except for mine ☺), we can quickly see the disappointment people face and their need to "get rid of" the dog(s) that "didn't work out." Our nation's shelters are overrun with these dogs.

There are a host of other excuses people use to abandon dogs such as:
- The family moves to those cities here in the U.S. that don't allow dogs.

- The amount of time needed to take care of the dog just skyrocketed.

- The new boyfriend or wife just doesn't like this dog.

- The dog doesn't like the new boyfriend or girlfriend.

- He doesn't get along with the cat, the new puppy or the goldfish

- He is getting old and it's time to trade him in on a puppy, or just dump him.

- He's too big for the new house (because dogs have a natural tendency toward expansion in smaller locations).

- The vet bills are too high.

- He barks too much.

... and we know this list could take up the next 50 pages.

Dogs end up in shelters because the expectation that the human puts upon them was just too much, and most importantly – people have not properly bonded with their dogs. The concept of putting too great of expectations onto dogs is one I will address often in this book. The issue of expectations is key in understanding dogs and in seeing why the human/canine relationship can fail. As the master communicators, we expect everyone to understand exactly what we mean by what we say. Yes, I said it correctly; "We expect everyone, even animals, to understand what we mean by *what we say*." Take for example a person attempting to communicate with a person from a foreign country. When the foreigner doesn't understand us, we simply

YELL. We can never grasp that the person didn't understand us – it must be that he simply didn't *hear* us. That same approach is commonplace when training dogs. We tell the dog to sit and when he doesn't sit, we yell, "**SIT!**" After that, we assume the dog is broken and we hit him, jerk him or, easier still, just drop him at the shelter.

Most dogs end up in shelters through little or no fault of their own. They are not broken or bad, nor are they stupid or imperfect. Often they are abandoned simply because the person who had them put little or no effort into trying to understand the mind of the dog.

Well-trained dogs are the rarest of dogs in shelters and are among the first to get adopted. The dogs that linger in the shelter are generally those that are out of control or sick and old. If we want to understand the core element that lands a dog in the shelter, we don't need to look any further than "the untrained dog."

Untrained dogs suffer from another problem beside their lack of manners; they also lack a relationship with their humans. Humans who train, or even attempt to train their dogs, form a different bond with their dogs than those who assume the dog should just "get it." The dogs who have suffered from a lack of relationship are sometimes more difficult to deal with and "re-train" than those who have some sort of human relationship foundation. We will address this more in the training sections of this book.

In order to understand why dogs end up in shelters, we need to look past the dog and see the human at the other end of the leash. It is their lack of compassion and commitment that is the curse of the dog. The dog could be just about any dog; he just happened to end up with this particular person, *the wrong human*. The dog is cursed by his luck of the draw. I've seen numerous dogs that one person gave up on, yet became incredible companions for someone else.

Truly bad, dangerous and unmanageable dogs are rare in shelters. Almost every dog can be trained – given enough time and effort. Finding a person willing to put in that effort and time is the challenge. Until we implement a policy requiring people to take part in some sort of training, or at least a pre-screening, innocent dogs will continue to end up in the wrong hands.

If you see a dog in the shelter and wonder if he can be trained or if he will make a great pet, chances are the answer is **YES** – if you are willing to do a bit of work. Some think that the work is just too much and so they opt to buy a puppy instead – these people really have a clouded and distorted vision. The amount of work it takes to raise a puppy is far more challenging than training the dog you get from the shelter that needs some fine-tuning.

It's my goal with this book to give a chance to those dogs that others gave up on – to give them a voice and a spark of hope through empowering people with knowledge.

Temperament of Dogs

To understand the *temperament* of a dog is to get a glimpse into the soul of the dog. Temperament, simply defined, can be translated as a dog's *personality*. Dogs have a wide variety of temperaments, just as humans have a wide array of personalities.

Simply put, here are two simple classifications of dog temperament:

1. Dogs that need work.

2. Dogs that don't need any work.

Dogs that don't need work should be networked quickly and moved out of the shelter so they don't begin to deteriorate, thereby burdening us with training more dogs than necessary. And, please keep in mind, it is only the very smallest percentage of dogs that will not be affected by the stressful kennel environment at a shelter. To allow well-adjusted dogs to linger at the shelter increases our burden because these dogs will then need some basic training in order to get them adopted. If they show up adoptable, get them adopted, so we can focus on saving more lives.

One of the key elements to address in understanding the temperament of a dog is what we call "DRIVE." Drive constitutes how dogs live in their daily lives. Some dogs are "high-drive", while others are "low-drive." High-drive dogs work well for dog sports and are often sought out as detection dogs, including drug, bomb and cadaver work. It's important to note that just because a dog *is* high in drive, doesn't necessarily mean that he is a natural candidate for working as a scent-detection dog. (Just as dogs that like to bite are not necessarily good candidates for protection work.)

A high-drive dog will run and run, play and play and almost never get enough. If you have a high-drive dog and hide his favorite toy, he will tear your house apart trying to find it. High-drive dogs work well in training because they always want something to do. People often get high-drive dogs for the wrong reasons. They think these dogs will be more fun to play with and will enjoy running and exercising with them. What people don't understand is that this drive often extends far beyond the running or play session they envision. High-drive dogs need to be occupied most of the time or else they can turn destructive – either to themselves or to your house. This information is covered in the section on "***Determining the Drive of a Dog and Understanding It.***"

Looking at the temperament of a dog is key to understanding him. Many rescue and animal rights organizations are opposed to "temperament testing" dogs, and with the low quality of temperament tests that I've seen over the years, I partially agree. However, even these rescue groups want to know what they are adopting: "Does the dog get along with other dogs?" "How is the dog with children?" and the list goes on. The behavioral assessment-testing guide in this book has been used to *fairly* determine the temperament of hundreds of dogs and has saved the lives of countless dogs condemned by faulty temperament tests.

If a dog has a "personality flaw", it is not a reason to condemn him to death, but it's a good thing to know before we place him into a family or situation that can cause him to fail and possibly hurt himself or someone else. For example, dogs that are aggressive with other dogs can do well in single-dog homes. Dogs that don't like their tails pulled or being run-up-on can do well with an older couple that is looking for a companion. In short, there *is* a home for every living dog; we just need enough time to find that home. I've proven this over and over again through the **Bound Angels *Shelter Angel Video Program***. In this program I took almost every variety of dog – from big to small, old to young, sweet to aggressive, and found each one a home or rescue – 100% of the time.

This is not to say that every shelter or rescue will have the same results; it is merely a statement that it can be done. Many shelters are dealing with the hurdles of space and time, and these hurdles are bigger than anyone on the outside can ever imagine. Doing the very best you can do is all anyone can ask, and reading this book, as well as my earlier book, ***Selling Used Dogs,*** will give you more power in this struggle.

Once we determine the dog's issues, through the results of the test in this book, we can focus on the best type of home or placement for the dog. Carefully screening dogs gives them the best chance at adoption into forever homes. We need to understand, as best we can in the shelter environment, what makes the dog *tick.* There are those who will say, "The shelter said this dog was aggressive, and see...he's not aggressive at all." I've seen it countless times, and to this I say, "BRAVO." Anytime someone can come back to me and say, "He wasn't aggressive like the shelter said," I'm thrilled. What concerns me greatly are the shelters/rescues that release a dog, saying he's absolutely perfect and then hear that this dog bit someone.

Getting an insight into a dog's temperament is not a guarantee of anything – it's merely a glimpse. It's better than nothing, but should not be seen as gospel. All dogs have the probability of biting someone – ALL DOGS. Don't think that just because a dog has never bitten someone, it never will. By the same token, let's be clear and understand that just because a dog *has* bitten someone, it is not a bad dog. Dogs are individual creatures that have good and bad moments – kind of like us!

Kennel Syndrome

People often adopt dogs from shelters or humane organizations and base their opinions on what they see at the shelter as to the dog's overall personality or temperament. You see a calm, sweet dog at the shelter, and you think he will be a sweet and submissive dog once you get him home.

I have evaluated, adopted/placed, facilitated the rescue of, and performed behavioral assessment tests on hundreds of dogs, from the most aggressive to the most submissive. One thing I can attest is that a dog's true personality will often be brought out only when he is in a neutral environment, not at the shelter. Shelters are far from neutral. The energy of a shelter is completely overwhelming to most dogs. This energy provokes one of two responses in a dog: *fight or flight*. Many dogs will completely shut down in this situation; others will act out in response. I call this **Kennel Syndrome**.

Kennel Syndrome is the behavior that a dog assumes in survival mode. Dominant or aggressive dogs can turn sweet and submissive in order to get the food or shelter they need to survive. A submissive dog may turn dominant in order to gain respect or shelter. Dogs are masters of opportunity and have survived as a species for thousands of years because of their adaptability.

There are countless ways a dog can land in a shelter. His owners may have abandoned the dog. Perhaps he ran away and was not found or he was dumped there. There are very few truly feral dogs in the shelter system. This means that a dog that was likely socialized with humans, living in a human world, perhaps inside a climate-controlled house, suddenly finds his whole world turned upside-down. When a dog lands in the shelter, all of this is ripped away from him. Perhaps his owners got sick of him or couldn't afford him. Maybe he got sick or got labeled "aggressive". Whatever the reason, chances are *it was not the dog's fault*. One thing for certain is that the dog that ends up in the shelter is confused and looking to make sense or to find a solution from what he is facing.

The things a dog experiences in the shelter are a huge shock to his system. It's like putting a human in a maximum-security prison. There is little, if any, human interaction in shelters. If there is, it's through the steel bars that house the dog.

Behaviors that are a part of *Kennel Syndrome* can include the following:

Cage fighting: Dogs that are kept within eyesight of dogs across the way in kennel runs will often get into and out of drive. Keeping a dog from ever getting to the dog across the way may foster aggressive behavior. Play barking can shift into defensive barking: "Don't come over here." And, since the dog cannot ever get to the other dog, the more aggressive dog feels as if he's winning. Then, when the other dog is finally released from his cage and walks by the stronger dog's kennel, the stronger dog is likely to become protective of the territory he's been *protecting* all along. Cage fighting stems from a territorial dominance, which is a self-protective aspect of survival. The more often this is reinforced, the stronger the behavior will become. This carries over to a dog seeing other dogs walking by his kennel. This is something to bear in mind when walking dogs by other dogs in kennels. If the dog in the kennel barks and guards and he thinks that his bark removed the other dog (the one just walking by), his behavior is reinforced.

An example of this in the real world is a dog that barks at a passing stranger. Each time the dog barks, the person goes away. This dog is learning, "My barks are making the person go away. I'm in control." If this stops working, the dog will take the behavior to the next level – charging toward the person. At some point, it may turn to nipping, biting and eventually attacking. The more often a "threat" is removed by an action *of the dog*, the more the dog's negative behavior is reinforced. Dogs with territorial issues must be taught that they are safe in the environment they are protecting – without their need to act out – and that people coming into that area are not there to do them harm. This technique must he taught by someone who understands canine behavior and who has the ability to be fair, yet firm, to the dog.

Emotional Shutdown: These are dogs that are completely turned off to the world. Examples of this are dogs that freeze and lay on the floor when someone wants to take them for a walk, or cower in the corner when someone comes in, tails between the legs, hunched over posture, etc. These dogs can be strong or weak dogs. What we see is where the dog's emotions landed him. It's similar to a powerful man crying in a corner. He may be acting weak, but physically he can still be quite strong.

These dogs need to be re-socialized through gradual exposure. Just the presence of a person near them, even if this person is doing nothing (in fact it's much better that the person do nothing) will start to teach the dog that having a person close to him has no negative implications.

Understanding this is quite complex for humans, but positive lessons as seen by a human may confuse the dog. For example: offering food to a dog in this state may make the dog move quickly for the food, which in turn may surprise the person and make the person jump. The jumping reaction of the person can shock the dog – and we know where that will land us. Just a few minutes of a person's energy in the immediate area of the dog is often the best solution to re-socialize the dog. Desensitizing "emotionally shut-down" dogs is best done by being in their presence with absolutely no expectations.

Spinning: This high-energy behavior is a clear sign of lack of stimulation – both physical and mental. It's most common in high-drive and working-class dogs – dogs that require activities to keep them busy or stimulated. Spinning dogs start by walking around in circles in their kennel, and the more they walk around, the more they turn. The turns are then succeeded by jumps, until eventually the jumps and spins bind together to form a behavior that looks like the dog is bouncing off the walls. Once a dog gets into this mode, it often leads to an obsessive-compulsive behavior that can be difficult to cure.

Cage Chewing: Dogs that chew at the bars of the cage are obviously fighting to get out and are often high-strung. The behavior can vary from trying to escape to an obsessive-compulsive behavior that takes a lot of work to break. This behavior also causes serious permanent damage to a dog's teeth, jaws and – depending on the construction of the kennels – often to his intestines, if paint and steel is ingested. Dogs that try to chew out of their cages often have been forced into enclosures and punished there. If the experience was a bad one, the dog sees it as a place from which he needs to escape. This goes against the instincts of dogs, which, as a breed, have little problem being enclosed in an area such as a den.

Overall Destructive Behavior: This can range from tearing up bedding to self-destructive behavior, such as biting at their own limbs until they bleed. This behavior can become obsessive-compulsive. A dog may look for attention and, when none is found, he will retreat into a corner and starts licking or obsessively chewing. Since most of this behavior takes place when there is no one around, it's challenging to pinpoint. Although this stems from boredom, it often surpasses a mere pastime and becomes overwhelming in the dog's mind. Keeping more than one dog in a kennel can often prevent these behaviors. Dogs are creatures that form strong bonds. Dogs that are left alone often times will turn destructive or anti-social.

Many shelters do not place more than one animal in a run because of their fear that the dogs may fight. Although this may be true, it's a bad excuse. Millions of animals are killed in shelters for lack of space, and for behavioral issues that can be prevented by simply spending some time in introducing dogs that can be placed together. This can minimize the stress of isolation and kennel syndrome. We must understand that with dogs, as with humans, isolation is one of the cruelest forms of torture.

Outwards Signs of Aggression: These dogs are the surest to be killed first in the shelters, as they are a risk and are the least likely to be adopted. This evaluation is done immediately when a dog shows any signs of outward aggression toward a human. Because it takes time to properly evaluate why a dog is acting aggressively, and because shelters lack time and staff to do this, the dogs are more easily killed. Often, dogs that show aggression are doing so out of fear instead of dominance. If a dog is afraid, he is likely to snap, growl or bite. If the person handling the dog is not able to make the dog feel secure or properly control or correct him, the behavior may become dangerous.

Food Aggression: Dogs in shelters are usually fed only once a day, and it's generally not the most nutritious meal or the largest portions. Keep any animal hungry enough and it will start to fight for food. It doesn't matter if it's a mastiff or a canary. An animal's survival instincts force it to fight for the sustenance to stay alive. It's a *kill-or-be-killed* attitude.

The Limits of Temperament Testing In the Shelter Environment

Many shelters and rescue organizations have implemented the use of temperament and behavioral assessment tests on dogs to determine their overall constitution. The problem with many of these tests is that they are highly *unfair* to the dogs. These tests are often performed by someone who was *shown* these techniques and may not necessarily understand them. Therefore they lack an understanding as to how to read the results objectively. Many people who apply these tests have no idea as to what the results mean if they deviate slightly from the answer they are looking for on paper. A dog may act aggressively the first time his tail is touched because he is surprised, but once he understands that no harm will come to him, he will let his guard down and allow his tail to be pulled and touched. Dogs may have a negative reaction to a poke on the hindquarters, but not to a stroke. Dogs growl and play bark, and often times this is read as "growling" which has a negative implication.

A huge part of these tests are the location where they are performed, who is performing them, the mood of the dog when the test is being performed, as well as several other factors. Dogs are very contextual. There is a simple test to prove this: teach your dog a new trick in your living room, then take him to the park and see if he will perform the trick the exact same way in the park as he did at home. Where a dog *is* mentally and physically – and what his immediate surroundings are – has a huge impact on how he will relate to an outside stimulus.

A very dominant, strong person can bring out a much different behavior from a dog than a person who is shy and nervous. I may be able to pull a dog's tail without getting bitten, but a small child doing the same thing might get snapped at. Temperament testing is at best a snapshot at the true personality of a dog at that given moment. A true behavioral assessment can only be ascertained by spending a good amount of time with the dog and addressing each aspect of the test in various ways and through various conditions.

Testing for food aggression is one of the stupidest things humans apply in testing dogs and in *humanizing* them. Countless dogs have been killed for this idiotic, unfair, humanized test. If a dog is eating, he should not be bothered. NEVER. If parents are too stupid to keep children away from a dog that is eating, they should not have dogs, let alone children. Once the food hits the bowl and the bowl is set in front of the dog, the food belongs to the dog. I cannot think of one good reason why I should have to reach my hand into the dog's bowl. If a qualified trainer wants to overcome the dog's natural instincts to protect his meal, there are a few techniques that I have taught and seen applied by qualified trainers that do work. However, testing a dog to see if he will growl or snap at a rubber hand is downright STUPID. I won't go into my litany of how this may be the dumbest test ever invented, but I would strongly argue to anyone that testing a dog for food aggression using this technique has no bearing on a dog's true behavior toward territorial dominance or resource guarding. Remember also that a dog living in a shelter will respond differently because of the mindset he is in while at the shelter. If we want to ascertain if a dog has food aggression issues, it must be done outside of the shelter environment and conducted in a fair way to the dog.

I've seen shelters test dogs for aggression by giving them a tug toy and pulling on the tug to see if the dog will growl. If the dog growls (and is of a "dominant breed") the dog goes down. The flaw in this test is that it's as stupid as punching a man in the nose to see if his eyes water, then stating that he's weak because he's crying.

It's a dog's natural instinct to growl when a game of tug is initiated. For people who do not know anything about a dog's instincts, dogs don't let go when you pull on an object. Instead it further enforces the fight behavior and the dog grabs the object tighter. Games of tug should not be used to test a dog for aggression if the only quantifiable result is posed as *growling = aggression*.

Determining and Understanding the Drive of a Dog

Drive is the level of energy that a dog possesses. It is also a gauge of a dog's persistence in the way he approaches things. For example, a dog with a high level of drive will try his best to climb a tree if his toy is hidden there. A low-drive dog will look at the tree and decide he can't get it, then just give up or go onto something else.

There are three basic drives in dogs: *low, medium and high*. Drive is not something that can be changed – it is the inherent personality and in the DNA of the dog. To take a dog that is high in drive and expect him to change into a dog that will just sit around and watch TV is cruel, just as it is cruel to take a dog that is low in drive and expect him to run and play for hours.

Some dogs may change in drive as they mature – that is, they get less "*drivey*" as they age – but during puppyhood and most of their adult years these dogs are prone to the drive that is ingrained into them. It's important not to confuse *drive* with puppy energy – they are very different. High-drive dogs are persistent and need to be monitored. Left unsupervised and untrained, they can become destructive. Puppy energy will dissipate as the dog grows out of puppyhood.

Below is an analysis of each of the three drives:

LOW-DRIVE - Dogs that are low-drive are generally content to sniff a little, walk casually around the park and then settle down for a belly rub. Given the opportunity, these dogs would just as soon lie on the couch and watch "Ellen" as engage in a fun game of Frisbee. When you throw a ball for these dogs, they will either ignore it or walk up to it and sniff around as if to say, *"Why did you throw this all the way over here?"*

MEDIUM-DRIVE – Medium-drive dogs are great pets, as are low-drive dogs. They don't expect all that much – they are balanced and content with life as it is. They like to play, but don't *need* to play. They enjoy a walk as long as they're on it and are equally content when you get home and want to watch a movie. They're ready for a game of catch (as long as it doesn't drag on) and are happy to be done with the game when you are. Overall, a mid-level drive dog is great for any person in almost any situation – and the great news is that most dogs are of this drive.

HIGH-DRIVE- High-drive dogs look like the most fun dogs at the party, but that excitement continues ALL DAY LONG. And if you think it's fun, you may be pulling your hair out when you try to get them to settle down enough to just relax for a little while. If you throw the ball for a high-drive dog, he will run up to it and grab it, run around the field, bring it to you and jump up and down until you throw it again. If you take the ball and throw it over the fence, the dog will either try to climb the fence to get it, try to dig a hole to get under the fence or will bark like a madman until someone gets the ball.

To determine the drive of a dog, there are some simple things to do. Find something the dog likes, such as treats or a toy. Show the dog the object and then take it away. I'll show the dog the tennis ball and then hide it behind my back. If the dog runs behind my back to get it, I move away from him, withholding it. He should follow me to get to the ball. I then throw the ball and watch him. Does he pursue the ball with vigor? Watch to see the amount of energy the dog runs up to the ball with, and the energy of his return. (Be sure you are doing this in an area with no other toys or distractions.)

Next we want to show him the ball and then hide it. Try hiding it behind some canisters or in a place where it will require some work for him to get to it. At this point we will see his drive. A *high-drive* dog will relentlessly pursue the object if it was something he was very focused on in the first place. *Medium-drive* dogs will try for a little while and then give up, and *low-drive* dogs will never look behind your back for the ball in the first place. If you have a high-drive dog and throw the ball into a field of tall grass, he may spend the rest of the day trying to find it.

The key thing in determining a dog's drive, as it relates to our work with shelter dogs, is to understand how he will fit into a home. High-drive dogs should be noted and placed with owners who understand the needs of such a dog. They are amazing pets and can be a lot of fun. They can easily be placed into training programs, including dog sports and obedience, and some are good for scent-detection work. It is important to note that high-drive dogs are the most common dogs returned to shelters because of misunderstandings by their owners. They seem fun at first and then suddenly become too much work. These dogs also don't fare well at the shelter. They quickly develop *kennel syndrome* and begin to lose sociability. It is best to keep high-drive dogs busy with such things as stuffed/frozen KONG toys, chews, or anything that can occupy their minds and their bodies. If volunteers are available, it is a good idea to get these dogs out into a play yard and let them burn some energy.

Just because a dog is high-drive doesn't necessarily mean he is perfect for scent-detection work. Most agencies have a series of tests they put a dog through to see if he qualifies for their training. The key issue with high-drive dogs is to place them into homes, situations or environments where their drive will be channeled. Unless properly channeled, this drive will be the dog's own worst enemy.

High-drive dogs may bark excessively and jump a lot, and because of this behavior they can be classified as unruly and sometimes aggressive. These misclassifications often cost these dogs their lives. Understanding the drive of the dog can save lives and get dogs to lasting, suitable homes.

The remaining low- and medium-drive dogs are the easiest to place. Low-energy dogs do well with families and seniors and any situation where not too much is expected of them. Medium-drive dogs fit into most homes well and are the perfect pets for first-time dog owners, as well as seasoned dog lovers.

I would suggest that an evaluator or adoption counselor ask questions of potential adopters to consider the drive of a dog as an important aspect to take into account before adoption. Find out what is expected of the dog and guide the people to the right dog. Often people are drawn to the "looks" of a dog and they overlook the make-up of the dog. This will be particularly important if people expect a dog to partake in activities such as sports, training and interaction that requires a specific drive or physical makeup. If someone likes the look of the low-drive bulldog and his goal is to go on hikes, jogging and play ball, this will be a recipe for disaster.

Not every dog is suited for every situation and it is important for us to educate, or at least attempt to educate, potential adopters. We do this in fairness to the dog and the people.

Questions to Ask Upon Relinquishment

Asking the questions below, and getting honest answers, will give us a better glimpse into the overall "personality" of the dog. It is best to ask these questions without any bias in order to get honest answers. If the people *dumping* the dog feel that they are being judged, they may sway the answers to what they assume we want them to say. The more honest the answers, the better we will know the dog we are trying to save. We can save our frustrations for later.

I suggest that shelters develop and maintain relinquishment counseling to limit the cases where people dump their pets for circumstances that can be avoided. For example, in many communities there are resources for free training, low-cost medical care and low-cost food available through rescue originations. If the people are having issues with something that we can solve without taking the dog in, we can save a lot of work and heartache. Therefore, spend some time speaking to the people about the issues at hand before you begin checking in the dog.

Questions to be asked:

1. How old is the dog?

2. At what age was she spayed or he neutered?

3. Do you have the current vaccine records for the dog?

4. Does your dog have any history of aggression?

5. Has he ever bitten anyone?

6. Does he like men and women equally?

7. Does he like children?

8. How is this dog with other dogs?

    a. Big dogs

    b. Small dogs

    c. Male dogs / female dogs

9. Does it have hyper, low-key or moderate energy?

10. Is he housebroken?

11. Does the dog like to go for rides in the car?

12. Was he an inside-only or outside-only dog?

13. How is he with cats?

14. Does he walk well on a leash?

15. Does he have any training?

16. Where did he sleep? Inside? Outside? In a bed? On the floor?

Evaluating Dogs Upon Arrival

Although I strongly discourage performing a formal temperament test on a dog when he first arrives at the shelter, we can do a basic evaluation to get a small glimpse into the dog's personality. This can prove valuable later when we do the formal temperament test, but for now we just want to see a basic evaluation. If the dog was an owner-surrender we have a bit more information to go on and this evaluation process is a bit easier, but for the sake of explanation, let's assume we're dealing with a stray – one for which we have no information.

- With the dog on the leash, observe his body language: Does he appear stiff? Relaxed? Withdrawn? Are his eyes darting around the room? How does he look at the environment and the people and other animals around him?

- Offer the dog a small treat. Does he take it, ignore it, take it and drop it or become withdrawn or assertive?

- Without speaking to the dog, gently pet his head and upper back? Does he move away, remain calm, stiffen, or snap at you?

- Make a slight clicking noise with your mouth and observe the dog. Does he engage quickly, withdraw, frighten easily?

- Have someone drop a clipboard or a plastic cup at a distance of about 5 feet. Does the dog frighten and withdraw, bark and snap, or startle and then investigate?

- Walk the dog by some strangers (assuming he has no known aggression toward people). Does he look to engage, get scared or freeze in place?

- Walk him by some other dogs and see his basic body language. Does he look to engage in a loose friendly manner? Does he snarl and growl with a stiff posture? Is he indifferent or aloof? *Be sure to do this at a fair distance for evaluation.*

Getting some initial readings on the dog will give us a scope of what we have to deal with and it will also be valuable later during our formal behavior assessment test. If the dog's temperament is changing drastically, we can at the very least know that the environment of the shelter may have something to do with his shift in attitude. It also gives us a baseline that can be passed along to anyone handling the dog. Dogs that are great on initial intake can also be marked in the system as "good dogs" and this information can be passed along to potential adopters, rescues and the public.

Matching Dogs with People

Matching dogs with people may seem like a controversial point, one riddled with problems when we are facing such an epidemic in our nation's shelters and one we may not be able to carry out. But there are countless benefits in placing the right dog with the right person. A dog properly placed has a lower rate of being returned to the shelter. One way to make certain that the right dog is placed with the right person is to understand the dogs at our shelter, and then ask the right questions of the potential adopters.

Some examples are:

- High-drive and dogs with strong personalities are not a good match for older, weaker or inactive people.

- Mellow, older dogs should not be placed with people who are active and wish to include a dog in their active lifestyle.

- Fearful dogs often don't do well in homes with young children.

... and the list goes on.

These may seem like common sense, but there are other situations that are often overlooked.

- Puppies need to spend time with their owners. Placing them with a very busy person doesn't give the puppy the right time and tools needed for proper development.

- Dogs with more needs, including those prone to illness or genetic issues, should also be scrutinized before placing them into potentially wrong homes. Can the adopters afford the cost of care for the dog and are they willing to commit to the expense and the workload?

This is not to say that we should become like those crazy rescues that never adopt an animal out because they are forever seeking the *perfect home*. We should know that there is no *perfect home; we* simply want to find the best home possible. That might mean a little pre-adoption counseling and some training classes if they are available at our shelter. Often people are willing to listen to advice when it is given in an unbiased manner. Even if we initially feel that the potential adopter may not be well-suited for the dog, we should remain open to changing our mind if it is necessary.

There are a few questions we can ask of potential adopters that will give us some insight.

- What do you plan on doing with your new dog as far as activity?
- Have you ever had a dog of this breed, drive or age before?
- Have you ever had a dog before?
- Do you have any other pets?
- Do your pets get along with other pets?
- Do you have any small children?
- Do you have a fenced-in yard?

- Do you plan on training your dog and, if so how and where?
- Is your landlord or HOA okay with a dog of this size and breed?
- Will your dog be an inside dog or an outside-only dog?

These are general questions that can give us an indication if potential adopters may be suited for the dog they are considering. There are no right or wrong answers; they should merely be seen as a guide. For example, a person may not know that a Border Collie is a very active dog when they see him at the shelter. We can explain this to them and if they understand that this type of dog takes a certain commitment, it may encourage them to become better pet owners. We want to be as fair to the people as we are to the dog. Counseling them sets a level playing field.

Why is this so important? Why not just adopt the dogs out as fast as we can and make room for more? Well, it is our goal to look out for the best interest of the dog and the adopters, and just getting them out the front door isn't necessarily a solution. Understanding who we are placing together will serve us better in the long run. Incorrectly placed adoptions can increase our recidivism rates and this can be a fatal blow. Returned dogs are generally more problematic upon return than they were when they left the first time. Education is a key element in reducing returns, keeping dogs in lasting homes and creating return customers.

* Keep in mind that a person can change for the right reasons if they really want to. I know many people who became more responsible through their pets and we should keep an open mind. If someone is very dedicated and sincere, giving him or her a chance is not the worst idea in the world. There are plenty of first-time pet owners who had to start somewhere. If possible, offering classes and pre-adoption counseling can develop these people into great pet owners and repeat adopters.

Many shelters offer dog-to-dog introductions with potential adopters' dogs and the dog at the shelter. This is a good idea and one that has many merits. There are, however, some shortfalls, the main one being that the shelter environment is not the most conducive to getting dogs into a relaxed state. Also, dogs that are possessive over their homes and possessions may act very differently outside of the home than they do in their homes. Doing introductions can only give us a snippet into the true relationship that can be developed between the dogs once they settle into their home. It is also important to note that a proper introduction and proper structure given by the human can make almost any situation work out. This is something we can determine upon interviewing the potential adopters.

Even dogs that have shown less-than-favorable initial introductions can end up living happily together. I've seen this happen in my own home and the homes of clients. If the person is willing, and capable of doing the work, dogs can adapt to almost any situation. The question we ask is, "Is it worth it?"

We need to ask some basic questions and take into consideration the life of the dog we are adopting out. The animals in our care are entrusted to us, and their safety and lives should be among our primary concerns. The simple step of knowing our dogs and striving to find out a little more about the potential adopters can save us a lot of work later and be in the best interest of the dogs in our care.

Most of these questions can be asked in casual conversation by kennel staff or adoption counselors. The process doesn't need to be a formal interrogation and it should never be seen as one. Training shelter staff and having open dialog is a great way to bring our goals to life. Kennel staff should have an ongoing dialog and relationship with vet staff, behavior staff, volunteers and management. An effective, engaging management structure will assure that all departments work well with one another.

Kenneling Dogs Together

Before I delve into the procedure for kenneling dogs together, I'd like to address a fact that is so often overlooked in shelters: the fact that dogs are instinctually pack animals. They function well in packs and live much healthier and more balanced lives with companionship. When that companionship is ripped away from them, which is what happens when they end up in a shelter, the weakened mind can wreak havoc on the physical as well as the emotional nature of the dog. Unless dogs are dominantly aggressive toward other dogs (something that isn't difficult to test for), they will follow a simple pack structure and will live together very well. At the very minimum, two dogs to a kennel will provide some companionship and stability in a kennel environment. The reprieve of having a companion in the environment of the shelter can provide a calming effect on a stressed dog. Without anthropomorphizing, I'd like to draw a simple analogy to human prisons. The cruelest thing we do to human prisoners is put them in isolation. No animal wants to be isolated.

A few simple steps can give us a glimpse into the way two dogs will get along before we just dump them into a kennel together. (However, I've worked with many shelters that just look for an empty space and put each dog into the next available kennel, and these shelters don't have an exorbitantly higher number of risk factors.) If time permits, I do suggest some simple steps to evaluate behaviors before placing dogs together.

Needless to say, dogs that are brought in together almost always should be housed together in hopes of keeping them calm in the stressful shelter environment – as well as the hopes that these "best friends" may possibly be adopted together. Although this is often not the case, we can hope for the best and we should always offer a discounted adoption fee to someone who is willing to adopt a pair together.

Overview guidelines to consider:

- For obvious reasons, placing unfixed male and female together is a bad idea.
- Fixed males and females can bond relatively easily
- Neutered males and un-neutered males can create more issues than two un-neutered males or two neutered males.
- Female-on-female aggression is some of the hardest to control.

Procedure for evaluating dogs to kennel together:

- Evaluate dogs outside of the kennel: in a play yard, on a walk (having met a few times).
- If possible, using a new kennel run is best. If one is not available, use the kennel run of the more submissive dog.
- Have both dogs on a line and walk them into the kennel (if possible using two kennel staff). Watch their interaction. Mild scuffles can be corrected.

- Hand-feed a few pieces of treats and watch the dogs' behavior.
- Drop a few treats on the floor to evaluate for the possibility of food aggression.

* If the dogs have issues relating to the treats, it's not a death sentence. Be aware that many kennel runs can be divided for feeding. If the option exists to work with those dogs with food or resource issues, please do so.

- Once we see the dogs do fine with us there, we can leave. If I have a question, I will leave the line on the dogs, exit the kennel and walk down the aisle. I will return once or twice and then make my determination. I then remove the line and move on to the next kennel.

* Be aware that dogs that are kenneled together should not have items left in their kennels such as toys, bones or food, as this is generally asking for problems relating to resource guarding and fighting.

Following is a list of legitimate concerns and explanations:

Safety of Kennel Staff: The safety of kennel workers, including volunteers must be a primary concern. Kennel workers should be aware that breaking up a dogfight is a dangerous task and should be done with extreme caution. I will discuss this later in another chapter.

When two or more dogs are in a kennel, workers should always enter the kennel to leash dogs in order to take one or both out. Trying to leash a dog at the kennel gate/door can cause problems – including the second dog running out. Using treats and a calm hand inside the kennel makes removing one dog from a multi-dog kennel relatively simple.

If there is a fight in a kennel, the worker should not enter the kennel unprepared. Sometimes a loud clanging on the door of the kennel will startle the dogs away from the fight. A person who must enter the kennel to break up the fight should be prepared. Please read the following chapter on breaking up dogfights.

Increased Workload: Adding more dogs into one kennel does increase workload, but that is part of the equation of saving more dogs. The extra work is not due to kenneling dogs together – it's due to the fact that you've probably got more dogs in the overall kennel. Cleaning out a kennel run takes about the same amount of time to pick up the mess from one dog as it does from two, or putting two bowls of food down instead of one. In fact, it's a proven timesaver to care for two dogs in one kennel rather than two dogs in two different kennels. It does take more work to move multiple dogs into other kennels when spraying down the runs, but again, that is part of the equation to save more lives.

Through using these systems, we will increase adoptions, lower the amount of time dogs stay in our shelter, and reduce the recidivism rates that plague shelters and rescues. All of this should increase staff morale.

Health Issues: Some shelters and behaviorists, argue against kenneling dogs together. The primary issues that come to the forefront are disease and the safety of the animals and staff. Since I am not a veterinarian, I won't debate the disease issue, but I would say that the risk of disease should not outweigh the risk of dogs being killed for lack of space when *that* is a primary reason for putting dogs down. If the dogs being killed for space are healthy dogs, my mind is perplexed that we use the "risk factor" of *disease* as an excuse for not at least giving these dogs a chance. After all, many diseases are airborne, while others can be transferred by people from kennel to kennel. Sick dogs should be kept in a separate area of the kennel/shelter to protect the healthy dogs, but using the wide net of "potential disease" puts many dogs at risk for no valid reason.

Safety of Dogs: Another reason that people are against kenneling dogs together, (also called doubling up or gang caging) is the safety of the dogs. Of course there are instances of dogs fighting in shelters or when kenneled together. This is why I recommend testing dogs to see how they will get along. But when you take steps to understand the dogs in your shelter, you can determine which dogs can benefit safely from doubling up and which dogs should not be considered candidates for this option.

Breaking Up Dog Fights

It is important to understand that dogs will fight, but just because they fight doesn't make them bad dogs. Dogs play fight and fight for rank struggle; they fight for food, toys and territory, as well as a host of other things. People argue - dogs fight. To think that you can put a group of dogs together and never have a fight is a dream. But there is a big difference between a dog that gets into a scuffle and an aggressive dog. Dogs scuffle and play rough – sometimes this *looks* like a fight and sometimes it *is* a fight. No matter what, we have to understand the nature of the dog and learn to work with that nature. Dogs left to their own devices can do many stupid things, which is why we supervise them, lead them and teach them. Dogs that understand leadership will look to that leadership when it's time to make a decision. That leadership can prevent fights before they start and it can also end fights and bring the dogs together again. Let's look at how we can best avoid dogfights and break them up if they should arise.

Allowing dogs the chance to meet and play in supervised situations will help them bond with other dogs and make them more social. The more positive experiences a dog has with other dogs, the better his outlook will be on future encounters. If he's had 100 good meetings with other dogs, his mind will think that the 101st meeting will also be okay. Then he will not have suspicious behaviors that could trigger aggression. I'm a stickler on making sure that dog-to-dog introductions work well and that, at any cost, dogs have good experiences around other dogs. I don't introduce dogs into situations in which I know there might be a problem. But, if a problem arises, I make certain that *I* settle it and that the dogs see that *I* settled it.

Furthermore, I don't take dogs away from another dog if they are showing aggression that can be worked out. Even though they may not play, they need to get along on a social level: no growling, lunging or aggressive behaviors. And if they show dominant aggressive behaviors, these behaviors should be settled before we part ways. Dogs remember their last experience very vividly and *that* behavior becomes reinforced. For example, if a dog tries to dominate another dog and growls at him, and we remove the other dog, the growling dog will assume that he got his way. The next time he comes out, he will resume his bad behavior. Settling unruly behavior should be done in small group interaction or one-on-one interaction – *before bringing dogs into a larger group setting.*

Please do your work when introducing dogs to each other in fair, firm and structured ways. This is immensely more difficult in the shelter environment than for family pets. When we deal with family pets, we know the ways of our dog as well as the dog that we are meeting. In a shelter environment, it's a guessing game.

The following section deals with dog-to-dog introductions. I urge you to read this section to prepare yourself before introducing dogs. This is the reason I am placing it before the section on introductions – a "*just in case*" situation.

When dogs fight, the two most common reasons are dominance or fear (considering that we eliminate stupid reasons, such as leaving a high-value item around, such as food, bones or toys). If we see any issue that might result in a dogfight, we should handle it before it arises. However, this section is designed to best break apart a dogfight. There are several NO's when it comes to breaking up a dogfight:

- **Don't** put your hand near the dog's mouth when he is biting another dog, even if you feel you need to do so in order to free the other dog. Dogs will generally bite whatever is in front of their mouths.
- **Don't** yell at the dogs. Yelling will usually only increase the dog's drive, which makes him bite harder. If the dog's mind is confused, yelling at him will not make anything clearer.
- **Don't** hit the dog on the head with your hand. His head is among the strongest parts of his body.
- **Don't** kick the dog. Unless you want the dog to turn and bite your leg, kicking is a bad idea.

Use caution pulling on a dog that has part of another dog in his mouth. If you pull on the biter, you can cause severe tears in the dog being bitten.

Once a dog is engaged in a fight, another drive takes over his mind that is difficult to interrupt.

Tapping, poking or giving a command is usually totally useless, as anyone who's ever encountered a serious dogfight will confirm. When dogs have connected, we need to minimize the damage (to ourselves and the *victim dog*.)

If we can analyze quickly which dog is the aggressor, it is best to place our focus on that dog. Once the fight has started it's often a crapshoot as to who is the aggressor or if both dogs are exhibiting dominance and fighting. If dogs were properly introduced, we would not put two dominantly aggressive dogs together in the first place. The dominant dog should be the primary focus of our strategy.

The further away from the dog's mouth you can remain during a dogfight, the better. The best place to be on the aggressor dog is at his rear. Understanding one simple piece of logic will give you an advantage: *A dog will bite whatever is in front of his mouth.* So, keeping yourself away will limit your exposure to being bitten. Some people will grab the dog by the scruff of the neck to immobilize him. This can work as long as you don't let go. Remember, your hand is very close to the dog's mouth. I don't recommend this technique – for the sake of your safety.

There are many *tools* and *concepts* out there for breaking up dogfights. Some include, cattle-prods, pepper spray, stun guns, garden hoses and more. We must be cautious not to cause severe injury to either dog, if at all possible. We must also focus on minimizing risk to human injury. Stun guns and cattle prods can cause injury to dogs – even death in some cases. Spraying dogs with a hose is often a common and harmless way to interrupt a dog's drive.

Once the aggressor has been distracted off of the victim dog, it is important to grab the aggressor, *not the victim*. Grabbing the victim may seem like the logical thing to do based on our emotions, but this can have dangerous implications. If the dominant dog is set on *getting* the other dog, placing yourself between them places you at risk. If you are spraying the dogs and they won't separate, get the water directly into the aggressive dog's mouth. It may loosen his grip, giving the victim a chance to break free. You do run the potential risk of drowning the dog, but if it is life or death, it's an option. Almost any step you take when breaking up serious dogfights can have implications of injury to the dog you are trying to stop. It is critical to understand that dogs, when engaged in a serious fight, are fighting to the death. So, if your intention is to be kind in breaking up the fight, you are bringing a spoon to a knife fight.

Another method to disable the aggressor dog is grabbing him by his back legs and turning him away from the dog he is biting – at the same time slightly rotating his body as if to turn him onto his back. This will imbalance him enough to loosen his grip. When turning the dog, be careful not to spin him. If you have his back legs, you want to move him away and rotate slightly in order to immobilize him.

65

Be cautious, because some dogs have a high likelihood of re-directing their aggression at a person. Even the most bonded dogs have been known to bite their owners during the confusion of a fight.

We should assume for this explanation that the dogs are wearing leashes or slip leads. This will make the fight a bit more manageable since we can control the dog without contacting his body. If two people are present, each can maintain control of their dog and watch for a loosening of the grip.

If you have access to a leash, you can loop it (end through the handle) to create a noose and attach this to the dog's underbelly, then take the end with the snap and attach it to something fixed, like a fence. Then give your attention to the other dog. This will immobilize the dog and give you an opportunity to deal with the other dog. Remember, it's best to focus your attention to the aggressor first to minimize damage.

This is a case of a pit-bull that clamped onto a small Corgi while I was working with a shelter employee.

The pit walked by the Corgi two times with no issues, but on the third time clamped onto the Corgi's neck. I could see that he only had the flesh and not the neck itself. I asked the person helping me to maintain her hold on the Corgi's leash as I worked to get the pit's bite free. I maintained tension in the leash without pulling (to avoid tearing the skin of the Corgi). Thankfully the Corgi remained relatively calm, but the pit's grip was a solid one. I tied off my end of the slip lead to a door handle. This kept the Corgi at tension. I then picked up the pit's back legs and rotated them as described above. When he loosened his grip due to imbalance, the slight tension on the leash allowed us to break the Corgi free. And by maintaining the aggressor's leash to the door handle, he could not lunge forward and re-grip. This endeavor took about two minutes, but it seemed like 20.

Re-gripping is something best avoided. Re-gripping or re-biting is when a dog loosens his grip in order to grip again and get a better hold on the item, person or dog in his mouth. When the dog goes to re-grip, we want to be certain that he drops whatever he *was* gripping, not bite harder and deeper.

Dog bites become more dangerous when a dog starts to shake whatever is in his mouth while maintaining his grip. Dogs that bite and hold (unless connected to a vital organ such as the neck) will cause less serious injury than those who bite and shake. It is generally the shaking that causes the most harm. If we can keep the dog from shaking his target, we have a better chance at minimizing damage. When the object in the dog's mouth is too large to shake, the dog will generally pull and tear, which can also cause severe damage.

The most important thing to remember in a dogfight is to remain as composed as possible. Do not put your hand near the dog's mouth in order to loosen his grip. If the dog does bite you, try to maintain a hold of the dog's head and if possible get hold of the dog's throat. Stopping the airflow of the dog will limit the strength of his grip and allow you to break free. Keep in mind that pulling your hand, arm or whatever is in the dog's mouth, is likely to cause some severe tearing. It is best to force the dog's mouth open or wait for his grip to loosen before pulling. Some people use pepper spray to deter dogs from biting or getting them to loosen their grip. The key thing to remember is to keep the dog close enough to you so that you can get hold of his collar or leash. At all costs, you want to keep the dog from grabbing and shaking.

Dog-to-Dog Introductions

How dogs are introduced to each other sets the stage for how dogs will interact with each other afterwards. As an example, I'll share a story about a dog that I rescued and brought home to meet my dog.

Boots was a dog that ended up in the shelter as a stray. He was a beautiful, long- haired SharPei (said to be about 3-4 years old, but I think older) and he was known for biting people and going after other dogs. I had spent much time networking him but to no avail. No one wanted Boots and it was killing me to think that he would be killed in the shelter.

Distractions, treats, toys, redirection – nothing could break Boots' aggressive drive. Plenty of people at the shelter had already wanted to adopt him but gave up because of his drive. I was stuck – Boots had no option besides the needle and me, and I couldn't let him be killed because of a lack of effort.

Boots loved me but would go after anything else that moved. The problem for me was that I had a dog named Silly that was the love of my life. He was the most important thing to me. When I brought Boots home, I had to work on the introduction. What I did was elementary.

I took Silly, who was very well trained and the sweetest dog, to the beach along with Boots. I tied Silly off to a post and had him sit as I walked

Boots by. Silly, being the friendly one, started, wagging his tail and went to greet Boots. Boots didn't like other dogs and went after Silly – and connected. I gave Boots a firm correction and tried again.

For the next seven days it was *"BOOT"* Camp. I never left my house without one or both of them and I kept an ever-vigilant eye on the situation. If Boots made a move toward Silly that resembled aggression, he dealt with my corrections. Between those corrections he was learning to experience love and structure for the first time in his life. He slept next to my bed, and Silly was up in bed with me. They ate in the same room and Boots learned to respect space when it came to feeding. It was a very challenging time for all of us, but we persevered. When Boots was good, he was very good, but when he wasn't, he was a nightmare. The occasional pop on the snout that snapped him back into reality quickly taught him that learning to stay calm and abide by some guidelines was well worth it. He got the best food, walks on the beach, a great home and a brother that he loved until the day he died.

My experience with Boots thoroughly convinced me that dogs deserve better than giving up on them when one training method doesn't work. Minute after minute, hour after hour, I watched their interactions and monitored and structured them. I reshaped Boots' entire conception of how to meet other dogs and people – sometimes through words, sometimes through corrections –but I never gave up on him, as did all the others before me. Some of the happiest times I remember are returning home to Silly and Boots standing at my door, with tails wagging in unison, welcoming me home.

So, to put this into practice –and this was an extreme case – we need to completely revamp the dog's conception of how it sees other dogs. If dogs have a drive that they can't control, we need to control it for them. If they never get a chance to mess up, they learn from the rewards they gain that compliance is their best option.

When I introduce dogs to one another, I do it slowly, deliberately and with focus. It always takes place with both dogs on a leash and I control everything. They need to walk by each other first, because I want them to know that I am controlling the introduction (and I will make sure nothing happens). I don't ever let two dogs meet head-on if they haven't walked by each other first and paid more attention to their human than they do to the other dog.

Once they've walked by each other, one of us (dog and human) stops and allows the other to walk around. I expect both dogs to remain calm. When they do, they are rewarded with treats and praise and we take it to the next level – the sniff test. If they do not lean toward compliance or neutrality, I will give a correction to the perpetrator. I will quickly and firmly get the dog to redirect his focus to me and to squash any nonsense that will get him into trouble. This can often be done by a simple pop on the leash to redirect. If the dog has a strong drive, he may need a firmer correction.

When I know the dogs will be compliant, I allow them to sniff each other for a moment or two. When that goes well, we celebrate with more praise and treats. We can then move to the next level – some free playing on leash. And when that goes well, we can play off-leash for a little while.

Again, I keep all things short. The shorter and the more positive, the more likely it is going to work out.

If at any time either dog shows aggression (and please understand that I am talking about dominance-based aggression, not playful growling) the aggressor receives a firm but fair correction. This generally starts out as a pop on the leash and a firm NO. We then try again. I don't believe in ending introductions on a negative note. That means, "If you growl or try to dominate that dog, he's not going away, and neither am I." If we're going to save a dog's life, he must get along with other dogs, at least on a surface level. I've facilitated the adoptions of countless dogs and have temperament-tested hundreds of other dogs; I have yet to find people who are looking to adopt the absolutely out-of-control dog with uncontrollable aggression.

There are the extreme animal rights people who will argue that correcting a dog is unfair and cruel, but I have yet to find one of them who will take these dogs we are trying to save in their current state. My best suggestion is to ask these people to join us in the euthanasia room, as we have to put these dogs to their death because the *"prescribed training methods"* didn't work out as they had planned.

There is no fate worse than death, and opting to give a dog a chance at life through a continuum of force in training is the fairest way to give that chance. Because one of the most common aggression drives in dogs is "dog-to-dog aggression" we must strive to socialize dogs in a manner consistent with a *minimum to neutral reactions to other dogs.*

When dealing with introductions, we don't want them to end on a bad note. Therefore, I prefer to get a dog into compliance before removing him. He must understand that his aggression will not make the other dog go away, if he thinks that growling, lunging or attacking works, he is doomed. He must understand that to live in this world, he may not have to love other dogs, but he's not allowed to try to kill them.

As I discuss in the chapter on **Continuum of Force**, we may need to move up a ladder of corrections and the correction must suit the crime. We can pop a dog on a leash in order to redirect him away from another dog and we can also use the technique of gradual desensitization, which is starting at a great distance and seeing where the breaking point is for the dog (where his aggression is triggered). However, in a shelter environment, where time is more precious than gold, these techniques are often not an option. The best thing we can hope for is that a dog can become good (or at least neutral) with other dogs with a proper handler and introduction. Many dogs that I've facilitated didn't start out all that peachy, but with a little work these dogs are alive, living today, because we gave them a chance.

The final two steps for correcting dogs who exhibit serious aggression toward other dogs are not for everyone. And, I would suggest that these options only be exercised when all else fails and the only other option is the death of the dog. I consider these techniques like a defibrillator that shocks a person who is on the doorstep of death, back to life. It's not pretty, but it may be worth the shot. If you can't do it, you're not alone. Thousands of dogs are killed because of personality disorders that people won't or can't address. These corrections must be done without anger or yelling. They are short, firm and fair. Their primary goal is to "snap" the dog back into compliance so we can develop a structured training program in order to save their lives. It is also a test to see if a dog will respect a firm correction and thereby become *save-able*.

*** When using the following techniques, it is important that the second dog be neutral. This will not work if both dogs are aggressive. We can't fairly teach a dog not to be aggressive if his own nature is aggressive and he is being threatened by aggression.*

Step 1: Using a very soft piece of leather or soft rubber hose, connect squarely on the snout of the aggressor when he shows the first signs of aggression. (Please read the section on Tools for Training to understand what items work for this.). Before doing this on the dog's snout, I suggest using the same amount of force on your forearm so you know how much *pain* it will cause. If done correctly, 80% of dogs will be startled into compliance. Some dogs will tune out completely to the other dog at first. If they do, I suggest allowing the other dog to walk around him as you stand next to him. It's not necessary, at this point, to coddle the dog – just allow him to sit and see that the other dog will cause him no harm.

** This technique is not advised with very small dogs, as you can possibly hurt them. I would not use this correction on dogs under 20-25 lbs. I would also suggest against using this correction on a dog that has re-directed aggression particularly toward humans.

Step 2: Using the slip lead that is around the dog's neck, you can immobilize the dog. I prefer to use a thicker rope than normal and I make certain that it is placed high on the dog's neck. I walk the dog by the other dog and wait for him to show his initial signs of aggression. This is usually a growl, raised hackles or stiff body posture. (Again, please be certain that the dog is clearly aggressive in nature and not fearful or playfully dominant.). When he begins to posture, I first give him a verbal chance by speaking the command, **NO**. This will either make him turn around toward me or remain in his posture (after which he will generally lunge in to attack). The moment he makes his move, I lift his front feet off of the ground using the lead around his neck. I hold him there for a few moments and wait for him to calm down. This technique should only be done by a savvy dog handler; it requires immobilizing the dog long enough to get him to calm down. Placing the dog back onto the ground too early results in an escalated aggression toward the other dog, or even the handler. It's imperative that the dog knows exactly what caused this correction to come down. In order to ensure this, I give the dog a stern "NO" as I lift him off of the ground.

To define this correction more clearly, I lift the dog until his front feet are off the ground. Do not yell at the dog, hit him or swing him around – there is no place for anger or emotion in this correction (or any correction). The simple idea is to "block" his negative behavior and immobilize him. It is not a punitive punishment or a dominating correction. Taking his mobility and air away is an attempt to block his destructive behavior. Do not use this correction on puppies or older, frail dogs. It is reserved for strong-willed, dominantly aggressive dogs only.

Correcting for aggression is not pretty, but it is with compassion that we do it in order to save a dog's life. Dogs that are fiercely aggressive are destroyed in shelters or forced to live in cages until they die. There are several steps to take before ever approaching the final two phases of correction. Anyone who jumps ahead to these two steps before trying the other methods is exercising their own egos. Anyone who refuses to use these steps when the others fails is simply giving up much too soon.

Dealing with Withdrawn Dogs

Withdrawn dogs are a common sight in our nation's shelters because dogs that are relinquished, abandoned or cast away will shut down emotionally and often go through a phase much like human depression. As we know, the last thing we want when we are depressed is someone to come along and play cheerleader. Dogs are much the same in this way. The other thing dogs don't deal well with in this situation is "over-coddling."

I've seen countless well-intentioned kennel workers and volunteers push withdrawn dogs further into *withdrawal* by using the wrong approach. That approach generally involves "explaining" to the dog that *"Everything's going to be okay."* Dogs don't understand English, or any other language for that matter, and more often than not get very confused when approached in such a manner. This confusion then pushes them further into withdrawal. It becomes a vicious cycle that is difficult to break and often leads to the dog's demise.

The best approach in dealing with dogs that are *withdrawing* or already withdrawn is neutrality: "I don't expect anything from you, so we're all good, just hanging out here." On many occasions I've taught volunteers to just *hang out* in the kennel with these dogs and do absolutely nothing – and I mean nothing. This approach is similar to the way we deal with desensitizing dogs to people. Allowing the dog to be in our presence without expectation allows the dog to *not fail*. We're not asking anything of him, we're only sharing some space and energy. There is no talking, no touching, no looking at the dog – we're only there in the kennel with them sharing the air.

As the wall of distance starts to fade away, and this can be seen by the dog's body language (softening of posture, looking toward the person, beginning to slowly move in the direction of the person in the kennel) we can start to change our approach ever so slightly. Grabbing the dog or making sudden moves at this point is wrong and a recipe for disaster. We want the dog to feel like *he* is opening us up, not that he is being *forced* to open up. When I am in a kennel, as the dog begins to move closer to me, I may put my hand on the ground and allow him to touch my arm or hand. I may place a treat on the ground 10-15" away from me and let him get it. I continue to ignore him during this phase. As he opens up more and more, I soften my position very gradually. I want him to make more moves toward me than I do toward him.

I suggest doing this over several interactions if at all possible. These interactions can be over a few days or over a few hours. The key thing is not to startle the dog backward into his withdrawn behavior. If the dog is startled and regresses, the progression will be limited greatly. A dog with a small positive progression will advance more rapidly than one with a jolted progressive and regressive (back and forth) approach. Using force to deal with withdrawn dogs is the worst idea ever. It will never fix the dog's problem and in the long run will only create new issues.

I often equate dealing with withdrawn dogs to helping children understand that *"There is no monster in the closet."* Imagine a child telling you that they are afraid to be in their room because they think there's a monster in the closet. Would you toss them into the closet to "prove" there is no monster in the closet? That is similar to the emotional impact of forcing a dog to interact with someone or something he is afraid of.

The best approach in dealing with the child is through compassion. First we could go into their room and be with them – asking them about their fears. Then we could slowly walk over to the closet and crack the door open to peek in. We could slowly open the door to be certain that there is no monster in there. We could then shine a flashlight into the closet and show that there is no need to worry. Eventually, through trust and compassion, the child would *see* that we were right and there really is nothing to worry about. This would do two things: Clear the concern that there really is no monster in the closet and, more importantly, build a bond of trust with the child so that future fears could be easily dealt with.

When dealing with the withdrawn dog, we need to focus on primary and secondary levels of behavior. We want to desensitize the dog to the primary issue and also form a level of relationship that will enforce a clear trust and bond between the dog and us (as well as future humans). If we over-coddle the dog or force his compliance, we run the risk of causing secondary issues (including mistrust or over-dependence). Dogs that suffer from a problem such as a timid personality usually have secondary issues that initiated the primary issue. Building up the confidence of the dog and his mental stability can solve the complexities that caused the initial symptom, as well as the surface issue that we are trying to cure.

Dealing with Neutral Dogs

Many people may ask, *"Why is there a need to deal with neutral dogs?"* The answer is simple: if we don't deal with the neutral dogs while they are neutral, they will eventually become dogs with issues. Neutral dogs are the perfect dogs at the shelter and should be the easiest to get adopted – providing they remain neutral. They could have a stronger core than the other dogs (those that develop issues, such as the high-drive or withdrawn dogs). We want to strengthen and enforce that core, keep them balanced and move them out of the shelter as quickly as possible. Keeping dogs neutral is much easier than trying to *fix* issues and can be a breath of fresh air for us after dealing with troubled dogs all day. Think of it as a playtime for you, as well as for the dogs!

We can reinforce the neutral dog's solid behaviors by constant interaction and validation, and, more importantly, we can use these dogs to help our other dogs. Provided that neither dog has any aggression issues or fear of other dogs, introducing our neutral dogs to those withdrawn and/or high-drive dogs can prove mutually beneficial.

I remember a high-energy German Shepherd that I temperament-tested at a shelter a while back. He was a good dog, but had lots of energy. I left him out in the yard after an initial evaluation and returned with a very scared and withdrawn shepherd mix. I held the leash of the high-energy shepherd and asked an assistant to handle the withdrawn dog. I managed the introduction and then instructed my assistant to let go of his dog's leash. Casually I walked Mr. High-Drive past the fearful dog and the gradual transformation was unbelievable. Within 5 minutes I dropped my leash and you would not believe the beautiful interaction between these two. The high-drive dog was happy because he had a way to let out his energy and the withdrawn dog was pulled into the positive spirit, and this soon gave way to a balanced personality. It's sort of like mixing hot coffee with cold cream to get a cup of coffee that you can really enjoy!

Over the years I've used neutral dogs in many ways to help bring about the personality of other dogs. The best thing about doing this is that it not only helps a dog to "get better," but by learning how to "be a dog" from another dog, it sets a positive image in both dogs' minds about their relationship to other dogs.

The importance of keeping neutral dogs *neutral* is as important as "fixing" the personality of dogs with behavioral issues. Do the work required through positive interaction, play sessions and training to keep these neutral dogs as balanced as possible. Ignoring them in an effort to fix only those dogs that we feel "need help" is setting the stage for the failure of all dogs.

If it is possible, allow play sessions with small groups of dogs, and integrate solid temperament dogs with one or two that need some exposure to "normalcy." This will ease the workload on staff and volunteers. Much can be derived from these positive experiences. If larger groups of neutral dogs can be allowed to play with each other, it is one of the best ways to keep them "normal" and prevent problems. Dogs function well in packs – allowing this natural behavior will keep them balanced, even when living in stressful environments such as shelters. It can be tough to make enough time for every dog in the shelter to get out and *play*. So, figuring out who the *balanced* dogs are and grouping them together will save time and increase the benefit to all involved.

Dealing with High-Drive Dogs

If you walk through a shelter and see a dog jumping up and down, spinning out of control in his kennel, barking, running up to the gate and back and forth, running through his feces and acting wildly, you can see the over-the-top example of a high drive dog. Often, these dogs are also suffering from *Kennel Syndrome.*

High-drive dogs are generally those that do the worst in a shelter environment. Everything that creates havoc in the mind of these dogs is exaggerated in a shelter environment. The slightest stimulus that triggers drive in a normal situation is exaggerated tenfold in the shelter. If a dog is high-drive in an open environment, he may eventually tire himself out in a yard or a home, but in the confines of a small cell, he will only drive himself crazy mentally and possibly injure himself physically. These are also the dogs that in homes end up confined in small rooms where they will eat through the wall and doors in an effort to escape.

Dealing with high-drive dogs in a shelter is a chore, but is totally possible. The key to doing so is to teach the dog that his "crazy" behavior is not what will gain his freedom, but instead *that* which will keep him confined. The common mistake handlers make with these dogs is they fight to get into the kennel, leash them as quickly as possible and then get them out of the run (oftentimes being pulled down the aisles) in order to let them run like crazy in the play yard.

There can be nothing more wrong than dealing with these dogs than using this *method*.

To teach the dog that he *needs* to conform in order to gain some playtime is the best method of bringing him balance. To begin with, I don't even open the door of the kennel while the dog is *spinning*. I wait outside and work to gain the dog's attention. Once I get a bit of attention from him, I give him a treat through the kennel door. I begin opening the door and if he again starts acting up, the door is closed and we go back to square one. Eventually the dog will learn that calming down brings him what he wants – freedom.

If I plan on leashing the dog inside the kennel, I enter the kennel and wait for him to calm (basically to stop jumping or sit in front of me). Once he does, I give him another treat, leash him, and walk him out of the kennel. On our way to the play area, I do periodically stop and ask him for compliance. If his goal is to drag me through the shelter, he will learn quickly that this is not going to happen.

When we get to the play yard, I again ask for his attention, which I reward with treats. If he refuses to give me attention, I will give him a correction using the leash and no verbal or emotional reaction with the exception of a NO command. I expect the dog to give me his attention, even to a minimal degree, before I let him run. When letting him run, I do so only with him dragging the line. Then I work on getting him back to me and rewarding him.

The key is teaching a dog that being calm brings rewards, and the primary reward at this point is his freedom and exercise. Bringing a dog into compliance and rewarding *that* compliance is paramount in teaching the dog to be more balanced.

If we feel bad for the dog and allow him to *act out* and "be free," we are doing nothing to help him heal. Every interaction we have with the dog requires him to understand what s we expect of him. If we don't teach him that, even in the short amount of time we have with him, we are setting him up for failure. Left to his own devices, he knows only the behaviors that landed him in trouble in the first place. People enjoy high-drive dogs for a very short while; they are a handful. So what happens most of the time is that people let them get away with the behavior, then when that doesn't work they yell at the dog. Some try hitting the dog because they become frustrated, and when none of that works, they dump him back at the shelter where he has next to no chance at a forever home. It is one of the cruelest things people do to dogs.

A dog's only hope for a normal life is to learn some structure through our limited interaction with him, so we really owe it to him, no matter how badly we may feel about correcting him. Our emotions often dictate our choices and dealing with dogs is no exception. Feeling bad for these dogs will not help them learn the behaviors that will get them adopted – teaching them what people expect will. So it may be a tough choice to make, but choose carefully. Temporary pleasure will not lead to permanent reprieve. I always opt for giving a dog the structure that I know will save him. I can inject fun with the structure by asking for a behavior (such as sitting still) and then rewarding that with a ball-toss – basically, *I get what I want - you get what you want.*

Be aware that reprogramming high-drive dogs is an arduous task. It can be as frustrating as counting grains of sand, but it is the dog's only hope at salvation. Getting him to understand that calm behavior gains him rewards will often create a carryover effect once he's back in his kennel. His mind will begin to learn that calm behavior brings rewards: *Perhaps I should be calm in my kennel.* That is why it is paramount to condition him to act calmly and to reward *that* behavior –not the jumping, barking and lunging. Bad behaviors can bring no reward in the dog's mind. As soon as they do, he will begin to depend on them and make *them* more and more extreme to gain his rewards.

Desensitizing Dogs
To people, objects, other dogs, and outside stimuli

Dogs that have not been properly socialized or have lost their socialization skills may be hypersensitive to outside stimuli – including people, objects, sounds and other dogs. Dogs in our shelters face countless issues, and over-reactivity to stimuli is one of the biggest. This book contains many tools to help dogs regain their normalcy. In this chapter, I will touch on some simple skills to desensitize dogs.

In the previous chapter on dealing with *withdrawn dogs, we showed that* the proper way to *desensitize* a dog to people is to do it slowly and fairly. In order to desensitize a dog to anything that troubles him, it must be done the same way.

The primary thing to consider is *what is the dog's initial reaction to the stimuli?* Is he fearful, curious or aggressive? A dog's reaction is generally based on his unfamiliarity with the object. That which he is not familiar with will cause his reaction and his constitution will dictate *how* he reacts. For example if a very dominant dog is spooked by a skateboard or bicycle, he will growl and lunge at it. A shy or skittish dog may run from it or cower. To introduce a dog to the stimuli is the first step in solving the problem. Most stimuli that trigger dog reactions are those that move: i.e., bicycles, skateboards, flags, paper blowing, cars driving by, people, dogs, etc. There are two concepts to the introduction of these items in an effort to cure the dog: **Flooding** and **Gradual Desensitization.**

Flooding involves *putting it all out there at once.* For example, a dog that is afraid of balloons will be walked into a room with 100 balloons and forced to walk through; if he balks, we drag him through – in an effort to show that the balloons will cause no harm.

Gradual Desensitization, using the same example, involves holding one balloon in your hand while you offer the dog a treat with the other hand.

Both methods have a place, depending on the dog. For example, a dog that shows aggression to another dog (dominance-based) can be *flooded* by walking him *near* a dog and correcting him for bad behavior. However, when dealing with fear, we opt to be a bit more compassionate. It will take a little more time, but it is worth the effort. Most fearful dogs will have very adverse reactions to flooding.

When my dog was young, anything that moved too quickly spooked him –skateboards, bicycles, flags – you name it.

The first time we walked down the street and he saw some balloons blowing in the wind, he panicked. I didn't make a big deal out of it, but simply bought a bag of balloons and brought them home. That night I hung one balloon in the room about 10 feet away from where his food bowl sat. It was simply taped to the wall. He was very curious about the balloon, but it wasn't close enough to interfere with his desire for food. As he ate, I walked by the balloon and moved it *farther* away from him. This is important – if I had brought it closer right away, it would scare him. Moving it farther away while he was neutral to it, made the balloon less powerful. Later that day, during another feeding, I positioned the balloon closer to his bowl. He saw it, looked at it and then looked at his food. It took him a few minutes to decide if he *should* eat. As soon as he walked over to the food, I removed the balloon. Again, he won. Since he was afraid of the balloon, it was important to make him more powerful than the balloon.

The next day I was able to hang a balloon right over his food bowl and the day after that I had several balloons on the floor near his food. It took him about a week and the balloon phobia was history. Now he barely notices balloons, and if they are around he will go up to them and nuzzle them with his nose. He's even popped a few without any incident.

The importance of this lesson is that we introduce the items at a distance and in a controlled environment. You don't walk the dog by a group of children holding balloons. That would be introducing too many variables –the children, the location and the balloons. If the dog is afraid of *one* thing – address *that one thing*.

I've dealt with dogs that don't like shopping carts. The cure is gradual as well. Allowing the dog to only see the item from a distance and keeping him neutral is key. A big mistake is to coddle the dog and walk near that item. (This is a common way trainers and others incorrectly try to desensitize dogs. The *item* in question should be kept at a distance; the dog should be walked, fed, played with or interacted with in a neutral manner around the item, and then removed without incident. The closer the dog gets to the item on his own, the better. We don't *force* the dog nearer to the object or person; we allow the dog to do so through building his confidence. And, we NEVER have a person that a dog is afraid of feed the dog or give him treats.

If a dog is afraid of people –or let's say specific people, like someone in uniform – keep these people at a distance while *you* interact with the dog. YOU give the dog treats and praise him while these people are around.

Another technique I've used in private practice is to have *good things happen when the bad things are around.* Simply put, if the dog doesn't like the postman, then every time the postman comes, the dog gets his favorite treat. One client had issues with her dog becoming scared when strangers came in and out of the house. I suggested keeping the dog in his crate and giving him a bone before people came over. The people were instructed not to interact with the dog during this training phase. After a short while, the dog became accustomed to *good things happening* and eventually began looking forward to people coming over.

Once we were able to break the destructive mental pattern in the dog's mind, we then moved to keeping the dog out of the crate and hand-feeding him some treats. Once he was neutral to this, we moved to the next phase and let other people toss treats to him. We eventually arrived at the goal of strangers being able to give the dog treats directly from their hands.

Desensitization must be a gradual process if it's going to be fair to the dog. Getting the dog to understand what we are doing will not work by *explaining* it to the dog, but rather by *showing* him. This *showing* takes time. Time builds trust and trust tears down the walls of suspicion.

Desensitizing a dog is often cleaning up someone else's mess. In the limited shelter environment we can only do the best we can, but rushing the process never saves time. Using fosters, volunteers and dedication to the process is the fairest way to help troubled dogs. There are no shortcuts to desensitizing dogs. Keep it fair and keep it simple. Be sure to understand the more neutral or positive experiences a dog has around a stimuli, the more quickly the dog will resolve his fears. By beginning this process, we are giving the dog an introduction that can be carried over after adoption.

Tools for Training
Slip-leads, choke chains, martingales, prong collars, remote collars, flat collars

In order to give dogs the fairest chance at overcoming the troubles that may lead to their demise it is important to use the correct tools. Choosing the right tool for the task at hand is crucial. Often, we see too much information or people presenting too many tools for a simple task. It's not uncommon for me to meet people who have so much equipment on their dog that both the dog and the human are confused.

This section will cover the tools and their proper use. Almost every tool that you will need is readily available at your shelter, local pet store or online. The key to this section is on the proper use of the tools more than the tools themselves.

Slip-leads- Every shelter I've visited has used the standard rope slip-lead, which is made up of a piece of rope with a noose on one end. This is hands-down the industry standard and, used correctly, it is the right tool for more than 90% of what is covered in this book. The exceptions, rare as they may be, are covered below. These leads, which slip very easily over the head of the dog and tighten around his neck, are usually homemade and use a thin piece of rope and often a steel O-ring. I've designed something that works a little better and is more comfortable on both the dog and the handler.

To begin with, I use a thicker 5/8" rope instead of the standard ¼" rope. . I get the rope from a marine supplier and have the handles woven into one end of the rope. (This is a surefire strong handle that will last – think boat ropes – they take a licking!) They may cost a bit more, but they last longer and when it comes to safety, I don't like to second-guess. Because of the thickness of the rope, these leads slip easily over the dog's neck and are less likely to cause abrasions on the skin of the neck. Some have asked if this rope is useful for smaller dogs and the answer is 100% YES. Just because the rope is thicker doesn't mean it won't work with a smaller dog. In fact, using this thickness rope allows us to use one slip-lead on *all* dogs. I see very thin ropes used on high-drive dogs and the rope riding on the dog's neck (and sometimes cutting into his neck) makes the dog even crazier. Thicker ropes have several advantages: they are stronger, last longer, are easier on the dog's neck, and are easier on our hands. The ring I use at the end of the lead is a 2" stainless steel ring. You may opt for a nickel or chrome-plated ring, and it won't make that big of a difference. I prefer the stainless steel ring because it will last a lot longer. I have a saddle repair shop make these ropes for me by stitching the ring onto the end opposite the handle.

Use of the Slip-lead- Using the slip-lead properly involves understanding how much pressure to put onto a dog and knowing when to "pop" the leash to prevent the dog from choking himself. Because this slip will constrict the dog's neck, we want to be aware that the dog, lunging ahead, is likely to choke himself. Most dogs in a heightened state will do so without thinking of the consequences, which is why we see dogs coughing and gagging after a walk on a leash or a walk through the shelter.

To use the lead properly, always begin with some sort of engagement so the dog knows where to pay attention. The dog should get corrected for lunging ahead and rewarded for looking at the handler, or at least staying close. This is simply done by first setting up some structure with the dog. If he looks at me, he gets a reward. Once the lead is on, we can "pop" the leash –meaning that we give it a quick, firm pull – when the dog looks back he again gets a treat. This "popping" of the leash redirects the dog to look back into the direction of where his "reward" is coming from. We want to avoid, if at all possible, the dog "learning" that pulling on the leash gets him to go forward. Instead, we correct the dog and teach him that avoiding pressure on the leash allows him to move forward.

If the dog has a good relationship, and the handler has engaged the dog properly, getting the dog's attention shouldn't be a problem. We can feed him a few treats as he walks next to us, to remind him where he should be.

The slip-lead is hands down the one essential tool that anyone who works with dogs in any environment must have.

Getting a dog to not lunge is very difficult in the shelter environment, but it can be a goal. The key thing to understand is that a dog lunging and acting wildly will begin to engage in other destructive behaviors. The dog doesn't need to be lunging at dogs in other kennel runs or other play areas. Our goal (the dog and the person walking him) should be to get him to walk next to us. The reward for walking next to us should include praise, treats (if possible) and continuing to move forward. The punishment for pulling should include pops on the leash to redirect, sudden change in direction from the human (which the dog will follow) and stopping altogether. Stopping should be done in an area where the dog can't self-satisfy his nutty behavior by barking at other dogs. We are trying to teach a dog that doing the right thing brings results – doing the wrong thing brings consequences. These consequences can be the withholding of reward, the refusal of the handler to move forward or a leash correction.

Choke Chains - It seems that choke chains and pinch/prong collars (described below) have received more negative press recently than anyone could ever have thought. This is due in part to the way many trainers use them. Remember that even a toothpick used incorrectly can become an article of torture. So, we must strive to understand the use of tools like the choke chain.

The choke chain, used correctly, will actually prevent a dog from choking himself. The choke chain is simply a short version of the slip-lead and allows the dog to wear the collar all the time. All we need to do is attach a leash to it.

One of the most important benefits of this collar is that it protects the dog from slipping out of the collar and getting himself into real trouble. There are many stories of dogs that have slipped out of standard flat collars and ended up injured or lost, and some dead. Before we start yanking on the dog's collar, we should teach him that the reward is about being next to us. That means rewarding him when he is next to us (treats or praise) and correcting him when he is away from us. In short, we want to put the dog into the place where he will get rewards.

Allowing a dog to keep constant pressure on ANY collar is torture for the dog, as well as for the person at the end of the leash. The choke collar allows a correction to startle the dog with a little more impact than a flat collar, therefore correcting him more quickly and more humanely.

The choke collar should fit over the dog's head but not be so loose that the dog can shake it off. There are countless varieties of leather, nylon and chain collars. They are all about the same – the preference will be up to the trainer or handler. Steel chain collars are the standard, can be purchased relatively inexpensively and also last the longest.

Martingale Collars- Martingale collars are basically choke collars *lite*. These collars are designed to tighten to a certain point and then not tighten any more. They come in a variety of materials, colors, sizes and shapes and work well for 90% of dogs. They are fashionable and reportedly safe in the event a dog *hangs himself.* (I cannot attest to that safety fact, but it is interesting.)

The good thing with these collars is that (used properly) they will prevent a dog from slipping its collar and getting away. This is the primary concern I have for any dog that I am dealing with. We must prevent the dog from getting away and causing harm to other dogs or to himself. Using a proper collar is step 1 in doing that.

Martingale collars work well in controlling most low- to mid-level drive dogs. I really like these collars for most dog owners, but think they are a bit challenging for shelter work. First of all, these collars need to be sized to the particular dog and taken on and off after each use. Most shelters don't have the budget to put a collar like this onto every dog. If your shelter has the budget, I recommend having one on every dog that will benefit from it. I do recommend that Martingale collars be suggested to everyone adopting a dog (as well as a name tag being placed on it to identify the dog if he gets lost). Choke chains should be recommended to stronger dogs or dogs that don't work well with Martingales.

Using these collars is similar to the choke chain, since they are essentially the same collar. Don't allow a dog to pull on them. Correct him back to you with a "pop" on the leash and reward the dog that is next to you – not the dog that is lunging ahead of you.

I do not recommend using martingales to "correct" dogs that are very high in drive or dogs that exhibit any serious aggression issues.

** *There are two types of martingale collars: those with a plastic snap-apart buckle and those that must be tightened and slipped over the dog's head. You will have to decide which you prefer to use, but be aware that if the dog is very strong, there is a chance that the buckle may break. The ones that need to be adjusted take a little more work to fit onto the dog.*

<u>Prong / Pinch Collars</u> – With the exception of remote (aka electric/shock) collars, few training tools raise the eyebrows of people as much as prong collars. They are seen as primitive items of torture and the people who use these collars are often scorned as tormentors of innocent animals. Nothing could be further from the truth if the collar is used correctly; in fact, these collars cause a milder correction on the dog's neck than other collars – if the user understands how to apply the correction.

These collars are most often made of metal and have prongs that set against the dog's neck. The prongs are dull and are not designed to "puncture" the dog's skin or throat. The pinch collar will only work properly if used by someone who truly understands it as a tool and not as a weapon. Some people will *cap* the prongs with plastic caps. This makes no sense since it takes the correction out of the tool altogether.

In order for the prong collar to work properly, it must fit snuggly against the dog's neck and sit high up under the jaw and behind the ears. It must be placed onto the dog by separating it (breaking apart the links) and then rejoining them once the collar is on. Many people use this collar incorrectly and start by pulling it over the head of the dog – this is wrong and should never be done. These collars are not meant to fit loosely on a dog's neck. The collar is on correctly when the dog can shake his head and the collar doesn't move or flop from side to side.

The collar should not be left on the dog for extended periods of time; it is a training tool that should be used as such. Used best, it is placed on the dog a short while before training and left on for a short while afterwards. I stress the importance of *not* putting the collar on the dog and then immediately beginning training. This teaches dogs to become *collar wise*. Dogs learn quickly that when the collar goes on, you have control – and when it comes off, you don't. These dogs will listen well when the collar is on, and blow you off once the collar is removed. We want the collar, as any tool, to become transparent to the dog. In other words, we use the tool to *teach* the dog, not to force him into compliance. By using training tools in this fashion, we can fairly train the dog with the tools and be assured that the training remains when the tools are removed.

The only bad thing about prong collars is the people who use them incorrectly. Used properly, this collar will give the dog a slight correction and move him into position more effectively than the strong correction that may be necessary with a flat collar or even a choke chain on a very strong, dominant dog. As I stated previously, no collar is designed to keep constant pressure on a dog. If there is tension in the leash and that leash is connected to a collar, you're making a mistake and not helping the dog. Prong collars deliver a quick "bite" onto the dog's neck and put him back into position.

Please note, there are prong collars that come with a *quick release.* Some people swear by them because they are easier to get onto the dog, but on the flip side, they have likelihood to break. On that topic, all prong collars have likelihood to snap apart when delivering a correction. If you are dealing with a high-drive dog, I strongly suggest using a *backup* collar to protect the dog if the prong should open. To do this, I use a choke chain or martingale and connect a small tab between the chain collar and the prong.

It's important to note that no collar will help in training a dog if you don't first strive to have a relationship with the dog you are training. The collar will merely be a degree of how much you want to yank the dog in order to gain compliance. I'd recommend that you spend more time focusing on showing the dog what you want through training than yanking him on a leash. Pulling on the leash is not training, and shouldn't be confused with training.

If the prong collar is used properly, we can use much less pressure on the dog than if we use any other collar, with the exception of a remote collar.

Remote Collars – Most shelters and rescues don't use remote collars, also referred to as shock collars, e-collars, zap collars, etc., because they are cost-prohibitive. Furthermore, they have gotten a bad name from the general public, as well as animal rights advocates and poor trainers, and many shelter employees are not familiar with their use or the benefits of their use.

Remote collars are truly the most useful tools when used properly. Make no mistake about it, most people use remote collars incorrectly. I've seen good trainers use these collars so well that training looks like poetry. Happy dogs receiving the slightest stimulation perform tasks happily and without even the slightest stress. It has been proven that dogs exhibit less stress when corrected on a remote collar than other collars – that is, IF they are used correctly.

Modern remote collars are so precise that they can be dialed in from 1-100 in 1-click increments. They don't "accidentally" shock the dog when the neighbor opens their garage door and some of these collars have a range of almost a mile. Correcting a dog properly on a remote collar can leave a positive impression and never cause problems in the relationship between the dog and handler because the correction is delivered without contact with the human. Also, it's important to note that most trainers/handlers will allow emotion to interfere with corrections. That is to say, if I need to correct a dog for doing something wrong and I am slightly upset, this emotion can carry over onto the correction. This, however, is not the case with the remote. If the dog moves out of place, a push of the button is *a push of a button.* The correction comes from the collar at a predetermined level. Because of the precision of the collar's electronics, we can dial in the precise level needed.

By using a "nick" setting, a dog can receive the mildest correction possible, getting him back into the place where we can reward him. These little "nicks" interrupt the bad behavior of pulling, jumping or acting out. The correction calmly and humanely corrects the dog without any emotional stress put on the dog from the human.

Some people use remote collars to "block" bad behavior in dogs, including aggression. I have done this successfully on many dogs, but don't recommend doing it before you understand the overall drive of the dog. Many dogs will "transfer" this correction to the other dog and thereby the "shock" will serve to enrage the dog even more toward the other dog. If a dog doesn't know where the correction is coming from, there's a good likelihood that he will take a guess. If that guess is the other dog (who he just happens to be looking at), chances are he's going to get more upset about that dog than he was a moment ago. When using a correction like a remote collar, we want the dog to be clear about what he is doing wrong and what he should be doing right.

Another issue on the negative side is that we can place a dog into total avoidance, which is what we do when we use a remote collar to "rattlesnake proof" a dog. If this happens with respect to other dogs, we run a strong chance that "our dog" will never want to interact with other dogs again and he may become anti-social. As much as I feel this is a very radical modification to put upon a dog, it is an option before death. I've known people who have owned dogs that would not let up on their aggression toward other dogs. These dogs would either kill other dogs or learn to avoid them completely. Since the people were willing to keep them as an only pet and would exercise caution in keeping them, this was an option. This is the rarest of exceptions because, as we all know, these dogs are killed in shelters almost immediately.

When training dogs, we want to decide on the best tool for the job, and understand the tool as well as the drive of the dog we are working with. Dogs that are *sharp* (those that excite easily) are best served with flat collars, martingales, and chokes. Pinch collars and prong collars are best used on dogs that are stubborn and those that don't spook too easily. The best tool that anyone can possess to train a dog is his or her mind.

Puppy Playgroups

The overall concept of dogs playing happily with each other is one of those sights that we, as pet lovers, live for. The romping, playing, chasing and tumbling makes us laugh and can entertain us for hours on end. Plus, it's a great way to get dogs good and tired. I'll address some of the benefits and concerns of puppy playgroups here. I have separated puppy-groups from adult-groups for the sake of explanation.

The *imprints* a puppy receives during his first 8 weeks of life are among the most important in shaping who he will become as an adult. Veterinarians, trainers and breeders agree that proper socialization during this period can be a *make-or-break* time in the puppy's development and will shape how the dog relates to children, other dogs, environmental stimuli, people and his world in general.

As I've mentioned previously, I am a big fan of kenneling dogs together at shelters and rescues whenever possible. The reason for this advocacy is not solely to make more room at the shelter (although that is crucial), but also for the mental and social benefits dogs receive from dog-to-dog interaction.

When it comes to puppies, there is such great benefit to expanding their groups, even among other litters. The groups should, of course, be monitored, and they are not likely to be without incident; however, they can be easily controlled and the puppies will quickly fall into line. Remember, a mother can control 6-8 puppies in her litter without much work, so as humans we should be able to do this as well.

There are many dynamics that go on in the groups. Keeping things in check will give us a well-balanced playgroup whose benefits will grow far beyond the group experience; it will shape the lives of each dog for his or her entire life. Puppies will do as children do, and should not be left to their own devices. Bullying is not tolerated, but it will happen. Showing puppies that you will not tolerate bullying will begin to shape their mind and teach them to understand that now, as later in life, bullying will not be tolerated – and we all know it's easier to control a 4-pound puppy than a 60-pound dog.

Puppies should experience several things in their playgroups. First and foremost should be interaction with each other, with humans and with objects that will stimulate their senses – including touch, sight, smell and sound.

Puppies will find ways to occupy themselves with most objects: among their favorite activity will be tug, and this will take place with anything that they can get into their mouths. They will determine who will win and who will play. A bit of rough-puppy play is not only acceptable, but also an integral game for them to experience. As long as the game stays on the tug and doesn't turn to aggression, all is well.

Hand-feeding puppies teaches them to respect the human's hand, just as they respect the mother's nipples. Of course, that requires the *feeder* to maintain control and not allow any *one* puppy to assert himself too much. Fair control is important and being a bully to the puppy or being excessively rough with puppies is NOT acceptable. Hand feeding puppies is best done individually, but it can also be a good exercise to put into puppy playgroups, especially when using treats. This can begin to teach puppies manners, such as waiting to be acknowledged, and pack structure. We, as the *leaders* of the group, will have to set the rules and make certain that they are followed. The puppies will look to the human for structure but will probably spend much more time interacting with the other puppies (because puppies are much more fun than humans).

During this time, we will have the opportunity to form good evaluations on the dogs in our groups. We'll be able to see personalities that would otherwise be overlooked. We will be able to tell which puppies get along and which will need some work. This is not the primary focus of the puppy-playgroup experience, but it is a great added benefit.

To desensitize puppies, as well as acclimate them to the *real world*, it's a great idea to place objects of various textures into the pen or play area. Many items are perfectly suitable for this experience. Try to think of soft things, hard items, shiny and dull objects, things they can pick up and obstacles they must crawl over, things that make sounds and things that move when touched. These items don't have to be expensive toys – they can be anything safe – from boxes to pans, to balls, ropes, old baby toys or towels. The key thing to be certain of is that the items are safe and can't be broken or swallowed. Common sense should dictate when the puppies need more monitoring, as well as when items in the playgroups are not working to the benefit of the puppies in the group.

Overall, the benefits derived from puppy playgroups outweigh most risks involved. The greatest risk that must be assessed is if the puppies are healthy, as certain diseases can spread from one puppy to the next. Shelters are breeding grounds for diseases, including parvo, distemper and kennel cough among others. Healthy and/or vaccinated puppies playing together limits, or at least greatly reduces, the risk of diseases. If there is a risk of disease, we should not risk the health of our puppies.

One great added benefit to puppy playgroups is the ability to add a webcam or a "puppy-cam" that can be viewed on your website by potential adopters. It's a great PR machine that can entertain people and bring in adopters as well as donors.

Dog Playgroups

Just as puppies can grow from playing together, so can dogs. Many dogs don't have the skill-set to interact with other dogs, simply because they've been sheltered from interaction at the developmental stage of their life. Dogs naturally know how to get along with each other; the bad behavior is usually something of an abnormality or something that is learned. It also can be unlearned.

In this chapter, I'd like to focus on dogs that don't necessarily have bad behavior, but rather those that need to get a bit more socialized. Playgroups are not about putting dominant dogs in with other dogs and hoping for the best. These groups are about bringing socialized dogs together and keeping them "neutral." Occasionally adding a shy dog to a small group can help him come out of his shell, but that is not the purpose of this section. Dogs that are relatively balanced can benefit from social interaction with other dogs and this interaction will serve to prevent them from developing Kennel Syndrome, dog aggression and destructive behavior.

It should be noted that dogs with resource issues – such as dominance over items or people or excessively rough play – should be introduced to smaller packs first and strictly monitored. Since we don't know the overall behavior of all of the dogs in the kennels, it's a good idea to get a general assessment first. This can be done by introducing dogs individually to each other and then adding another dog to the group. The assessment of a small group will give us a sense of whether dogs of that group can be brought into another group.

Bringing groups of dogs together begins with understanding the behavior of the dogs we are introducing. We focus on bringing neutral dogs with neutral dogs. If there is a majority of neutral dogs, the pack will thrive in neutrality. Weaker or dominant dogs can be brought into the pack once they've had some behavior training. Do not introduce dominant dogs into a pack of neutral dogs; playgroups are only for dogs that know how to get along in a pack. Trying to solve one dog's problems by introducing him into a good pack is not something for the average person to undertake.

I strongly advise against the concept of letting *dogs train dogs,* as some other trainers do. Everything that happens to the dog in my care is because of ME, not because another dog is asserting himself. In fact, the only alpha in my pack is *ME.* Dogs don't work things out around me; I work things out for them. Taking this attitude takes pressure off of the dogs and makes the group experience much more balanced.

So, putting aside the issues of dominance, fear, possessiveness and anything else, we can certainly find a good group of dogs at any shelter that will benefit from social dog-on-dog interaction. These dogs will remain social and will grow into better dogs through playtime and playgroups. A group of dogs running around is a great way to inject positive experiences into their stay at the shelter and a good way to tire them out.

When dogs play in the yard, I like to see how they react with some very low-level toys. Food and high-level objects should not be a part of any dog playgroups.

Aside from the benefits that the dogs receive from this interaction, potential adopters enjoy seeing a group of dogs playing; they can then imagine the dogs doing the same at their homes. And, since we do strive for manners during play, we can assure that the dogs are learning as they play. Dogs living at shelters face a great deal of stress every day and generally only have very limited interaction with people, as well as with other dogs. We strive to alleviate many issues by use of these groups, including: exercise, relieving stress, increasing sociability – as well as just having fun. Dogs that learn to get along in playgroups have a much better chance at adoption and a reduced rate of recidivism. Everyone wants a dog that gets along with other dogs. Using the groups as a way to exercise and train dogs will also free up time to spend on more *troubled* dogs.

I encourage shelters to use volunteers to bring small groups of dogs together for play during times such as kennel cleaning. Volunteers should be relatively dog- savvy people and should never be given more dog(s) than they can handle. Volunteers should have some basic understanding of dog behavior and be physically able to handle the dogs in their care. If possible, it is best to have two volunteers monitor groups of dogs, for obvious reasons – including breaking up potential fights.

One of the best reasons to group dogs into small groups is more *bang for the buck*. One volunteer can handle one dog; two volunteers should be able to handle 4-5 dogs or more, once the dogs are comfortable in dog playgroups.

The Importance of Training Programs for the Public at Shelters

Developing a training program at a shelter is one of the best moves that a shelter can make, for several reasons. The most important reason is it gives you a built-in PR machine. People who see shelters as the place to go for resources – to adopt a dog and to train the dog they got from you – will be less likely to dump their dogs. Shelters that have behavioral programs enjoy higher adoptions, fewer returns and are seen as a positive addition to their community – the old *dogcatcher* label can never be further removed than from a shelter that offers dog training to adopters. Some shelters even offer training programs for dogs that were *not* adopted from their shelter. This is a decision that should be made by the shelter director.

Volunteers can participate and use the training program to work with the dogs living at the shelter and make these dogs much more adoptable. Volunteers who are able to *work with* dogs usually feel that they are fulfilling a big void in the dog's life – and they're right. That is most often the reason people want to volunteer at shelters. The trainer, aside from providing classes for adopters, should also offer basic dog obedience classes for shelter volunteers. This can be done once or twice a week using dogs that are currently living at the shelter. Determining if shelter dogs should participate in the training or if they should have separate classes, is something that should be left up to the training director. Some trainers will want to do a brief evaluation of the dogs that will participate in a group class. This is totally acceptable and a very good idea.

Training programs are easy and cost effective to set up. Many local trainers will welcome the opportunity to offer a free or low cost 4-6 week class (1-2 times weekly) in hopes of helping the shelter and promoting their own business. Apprentice trainers can prove beneficial for most basic training. The cost of a training program, if there is one, can be offset through fees paid by dog owners participating in the program. One great idea is to incorporate a fee into the *new adoption fee* and refund it when the course is complete.

For example, add $100 to the adoption fee. Make the adopter is aware that this fee will be refunded when the dog and owner complete the 4-week course. Those that don't complete the course forfeit the fee. The public will also be willing to pay a small fee for training their dogs at the shelter, knowing they are helping to save more dogs through their participation, as well as the benefits of training their dogs.

There are countless benefits for offering a training program at local shelters and NO downsides. Getting people into shelters is, after all, one of the primary problems we face today. People see shelters as a place to go to *dump* dogs, not a place for training. Changing that image is imperative if we want to save more dogs. The shelter should be seen as a resource, not a gloom-and-doom depressing place.

Training programs at shelters should focus only on basic training, such as leash walking, simple exercises such as sit, stay, come, down, etc. There is generally not enough space or interest to move past basic obedience in all but a very few shelters.

Another great thing that will be accomplished through proper training is dog-to-dog socialization, and for this reason adult dogs and puppies should be separated into two different programs. Determining the age of the dogs in the different groups should be left up to the trainer, but as a rule of thumb dogs less than 9-12 months will be in the puppy program.

The program's duration need not be longer than 6 weeks, but should not be shorter than 4-5 sessions. We want people to walk away with a basic understanding of dog training, and this won't happen in one or two sessions. We also want to help people form a stronger bond with their dog and minimize the risk of recidivism.

Dogs that are trained are better members of society and those people who train their dogs form stronger bonds and are more likely to keep their dogs in adverse times. A good trainer can motivate students: both human and canine.

The Binary Dog

If you are reading this on your computer, you are aware of the unlimited power that your computer holds. It can compute complicated numerical equations, edit 3-D movies, compose a symphony, play complex video games, and write simple letters. In fact, some of you may be reading this on a phone or tablet that can do the same. All of these things are accomplished with a simple basic starting point, *1's and 0's*. All of the most complicated things that your computer does are broken down into 1's and 0's and through this basic fundamental system, all of the complex things your computer does can be accomplished. This is called the *binary code*.

Training a dog and understanding how a dog thinks can be broken down just as simply.

Your dog lives in the black and white. If we wish to understand our dogs better and communicate better with them, we need to walk in the middle. Many people think this *middle* is the grey, but it's not– it is the line *between* the black and white. It is the point upon which we stand that allows us to jump from black *to* white without hesitation. In fact, it is neither black nor white, but the place of choice.

To break this concept down into rudimentary terms, let's start our inter-species communication with the binary code of *YES* and *NO*. If the dog does something we like or approve of, we say YES and give the dog a treat to reinforce that the *YES* is a positive. Since dogs do not speak English, we will teach them through the use of a reward (i.e., treat)" that YES is good. By the same token, we need to teach the dog that NO is disapproval, and in order to do that we will withhold the reward (sort of a punishment).

Simple:

YES is good. GOOD = Reward
NO is "not" good. NOT GOOD = No Reward

A simple way to put this method into play is to watch a dog that is exhibiting negative behavior – for example jumping or barking. As long as the dog jumps and barks, we do not reward the dog. Contrary to the belief that yelling NO will make him stop. Yelling at a dog is a reinforcement that may put the dog further into *drive*. Instead of adding to the negative behavior, we can ignore the dog's action by not giving him reinforcement, such as yelling or hitting. Even a negative reinforcement such as yelling, hitting, or squirting a dog with water can, and does, serve as a type of reinforcement in his mind – be it negative or positive.

If a dog is exhibiting a powerful drive such as aggression, this method will probably not work, but this binary communication technique will develop the building blocks of communication instead of solutions to complex behaviors. I would add that by using building blocks now, complex behaviors will be much easier to solve later on.

When a dog is jumping, we simply wait for the dog to stop the behavior and say YES. Then give the dog a treat. The dog instantly starts to relate that the word YES and the treat mean the same thing - APPROVAL. When starting out with dogs that are not exhibiting negative behaviors, we can simply give the dog a treat and a YES for looking at us, sitting or being calm. After all, calm behavior is something we want to reward. Most people enforce the negative with NO's and OFF. If we focus on rewarding positive behaviors, dogs will be more likely to offer them.

The *binary* approach is the simplest method for the dog to understand, and the easiest for us to apply. Instead of trying to get the dog to understand that you are upset because of his actions and trying to make him do what you want him to do, it becomes a matter of – 1's and 0's - **YES** or **NO.** You either like what the dog is doing or you don't.

If you like what your dog is doing, he gets a treat and a YES,
If you don't like it, he gets nothing and a short NO.

It's important to note that the NO is not a firm, yelling or angry NO. It's more of a *NOPE*. If you put too much emphasis on the NO, it starts to carry more weight than the YES. Remember, it's the way we say things that the dog understands – more so that what we are actually saying. If we yell the NO, *that* is reinforcement in and of itself. The YES must carry more of a meaning and can be a happy-jolly-excited YES. Many times women will have an easier time adding emotion and men will have an easier time expressing disappointment. It is important for us to balance our emotions when it comes to dog training. This means expressing ourselves in a way the dog can understand.

Dogs live in the present and if we truly understand *that*, we can appreciate that we must reward or punish in the NOW. If a dog did something negative or positive even five seconds ago, the NOW is gone. If a dog is jumping and stops for a second –reward that action NOW with an enthusiastic YES and a treat. Also, if a dog makes a movement toward a negative behavior and doesn't follow through – for example he goes for your favorite shoe and you say NO and he stops, reward *that* immediately. If you don't praise his accomplishments as soon as they happen, you're not rewarding the positive steps. Your dog can get confused if you don't include the YES *and* the NO. Using only YES' gives a dog a one-sided perspective as to what you want or expect.

People often think that dogs can be trained in either a solely positive or purely corrective training method – this could not be further from the truth. Although I don't agree with over-correcting dogs, I do believe that a firm correction, properly placed, is not only fair but also necessary when dealing with certain negative behaviors. Remember, dogs live in the black and white. They understand that there is a payment or punishment for each and every one of their actions.

When setting out to train a dog or changing his behavior, we need to start with the basics of the *binary system*. We need to lead the dog along the path of what he is doing and find his stumbling blocks. As we approach each stumbling block, we need to teach the dog positive and negative. If he's heading in a direction that we like, we approve and reward – if he's heading in a direction that we don't like, we disapprove and punish. (In most cases the punishment need not be more severe than the withholding of praise or reward.). This method can be used to lure and shape behaviors by rewarding *little steps* along the way to complex exercises. At each step, we reward the dog for the movement or action that is positive, and later we can chain these actions together by withholding the intermittent rewards for an ultimate reward at the end of the completed task.

Using this simple approach to training your dog will give you an advantage to understanding how to shape behaviors into those that you like. It can be a fun game to play with your dog on a daily basis. I use this approach in almost every situation I'm called upon to fix.

- When it's time for a walk, the leash doesn't get attached to the collar until the dog is calm and sitting down.
- If my dog tries to run out the door ahead of me, I close the door.

- I don't put my dog's food down until he sits and waits.
- My dog doesn't get petted until he sits calmly in front of me.
- I don't open the door to my dog's crate if he's crying or carrying on.

All of these exercises are part of the *binary code* of YES and NO. No matter how complex something may seem, remember it's made up of two simple things – YES and NO. Focus on the positive aspect and reward it. Shape the negative toward the positive and start to reward *that*. Eventually you will begin to see all behaviors as 1's and 0's - YES' and NO's.

I believe that all training should be fair to the dog. Since the dog has an unfair disadvantage in that we are trying to teach him *our* system, we must strive to make learning easy and fun for him. Giving a dog only two directions to move toward makes the path much clearer than a complex expectation. Remember, your dog doesn't know what you want if you don't teach him. Don't expect your dog to be a mind reader. Whether you are approaching the training of your first dog or you have had dogs your entire life, try using the *binary system* and see how fair training can be for both you and your dog.

Relationship over Training

This section is a modification of an online article I wrote entitled ***Building a Relationship Before You Start Training***. I find it is highly unfair that trainers, and people in general, begin training a dog that has no idea of who we are and what we want. It's like a stranger walking up to you and asking you to carry his groceries, and when you don't comply he gets upset with you and yells at you and hits you. Dogs need to understand what we expect of them and this can easily be set up through a small amount of work in *building a relationship* with them. This can take anywhere from a few short minutes giving the dog treats to a long time in teaching the dog that we mean him no harm. It will depend on the individual dog and we should watch for the dog's signals that he is relating to us and is open to training. The signs I look for are willingness to engage, seeking to interact, actually interacting, and offering behaviors such as sit and down.

The very first thing a dog needs when he is introduced into a new pack or family is structure. That structure includes everything the dog experiences in the home and in his training. I should add that it makes little difference if this is a puppy or a full-grown dog. I am in favor of giving a dog exactly what he needs to be safe and happy... all of this begins with structure.

The dog needs to know where he belongs and what is expected of him. He needs to know right from wrong, and NEVER be punished for doing something that he was not made aware was wrong and clearly understood it. This includes not *forcing* a dog to sit, stay, come, heel, not correcting a dog for having an accident, etc. FIRST you teach the dog what you want him to know, and then you make sure he knows what it is, and then you may correct him if he is not following the rules. Corrections in the dog-world do not involve emotion and don't ever carry a grudge. You do not yell at a dog or stay mad after the correction has been made. You also should not coddle the dog afterwards, as this sends a very mixed signal to the dog.

Structure gives the dog permission to let down his guard and gives him a crystal- clear picture of who is in charge. To start with, who feeds him and who walks him? In the shelter environment we don't have this system of structure, but instead we develop the beginning phases of this part by using treats or play. Dogs need structure before love. A dog that respects you will love you more than a dog that solely loves you. Dogs look to a leader for protection and guidance, but not necessarily love.

One of the best things for a dog is to receive limited freedom during training, so playtime should only take place after we are done with training. Allowing a dog to play and then confining him to training is unfair and will make for a reluctant participant. A dog that is brought to training from the confinement of a kennel, crate or even a room will see the training as a form of freedom. Once done with training, we can allow the dog some playtime and freedom as a further reward.

Training should be done with the use of a long-line (10+ foot canvas or nylon line) and the training should be structured. Even playing in the beginning should take place on a line that controls the dog's ability to run away, thereby forcing you to chase him. Keep it simple for the dog to focus on you. If he turns away from you, move and gain his attention. When he starts to follow you again, reward him with either praise or a treat.

Many people who do not understand dogs, trainers included, make the mistake of putting human traits and emotions onto their dogs. If you really love your dog, you will educate yourself to learn how a dog thinks and what the dog needs to be happy. The single most important thing that will achieve this *happiness* is *structure*. Structure, in a dog's eyes, is as important as food. If you'd consider it cruel to deprive your dog of food, then realize you may be doing the same by depriving him of structure.

Once the dog has a clear understanding of structure and builds a relationship with his human companion, he can begin training. Training without a relationship will accomplish very little, and what is does accomplish is not built out of respect. The dog may sit, come, heel or whatever, but he is not doing it out of a solid groundwork. To be fair in training, you have to prove yourself as a fair leader. A dog will follow with vigor a fair and strong leader.

If your goal is to build a relationship based on love and understanding, take the time to build a solid groundwork with your dog before you begin training. A relationship with your dog will last his entire life. Making careless mistakes in the beginning will carry through the dog's entire life. A little planning is worth the results that it will create. Every interaction with a dog is a small but significant imprint on how he will see the world.

One of the very first things I do with a new dog is *Engagement Training.* Engagement Training is a system of playing with the dog and allowing him to derive a certain amount of pleasure through praise, playtime, treats or other rewards. But all of these positive experiences have one thing in common – they relate right back to me and my relationship with the dog.

In its simplest terms, I reward the dog for looking at me and interacting with me. I have a long line on the dog's collar and every time he looks at me, I give him a treat or start to play a game of tug. It is best to keep engagement training limited to food rewards in the initial phases. I stand in front of the dog and wait for him to look at me and when he does, I say YES and give him a reward or treat. If he wanders off (he can't go too far because of the line), I wait till he wanders back and reward him. Eventually the dog will only look to me. I don't use the line to *yank* the dog back to me; I simply step on it to keep him from moving too far away. When he *self-corrects* and looks at me, I re-engage him and start the game again.

When the dog first leaves the kennel, it is likely that he will ignore you and pay more attention to all the stimuli in the surrounding kennels and yards. Allow this to run its course until you are ready to start your session with him in the play/training area. This training is best done before feeding, since we are using food treats, and an empty stomach will be much easier to lure with food rewards. Furthermore, if the training is done properly and we end on a good note and walk him back to his kennel, and shortly thereafter his dinner shows up, he receives a double reward. In either case, try to do all training before mealtime.

Once we have a dog that is looking to us for treats and is sincerely interested in us, we are ready to do almost any sort of training. We can now withhold the treats or reward until we get what we want. It's simple logic: the dog knows we have something he wants; now it's fair to ask him to do something to get it.

If every experience with the dog can be short and beneficial, the dog will succeed much more rapidly than training to failure. The common mistake is to train to failure. Even if different people are interacting with the dog on different days, the dog will see the interaction itself as a learning experience. The key to these engagement and relationship-building exercises is to make being around humans fun.

If playtime for the dog involves playing with other dogs, it is a good idea to structure our *training* before the playtime with the other dogs. Without a doubt, playing with other dogs is a lot more fun than having to pay attention to a human, so we want the dog to understand that we even control the playtime. By doing this, and withholding the playtime, we teach the dog that structure brings freedom. Pulling a dog away from another dog to train him is not productive for us and certainly not fun for him.

The Training Scenario for Shelter Dogs

As much as I would like to think that every dog at a shelter arrives at Club Med and is going to get the perfect training regimen his entire time there, I understand the reality. If you are reading this book and work at a shelter that is able to provide unlimited training time for your dogs, you are in the very small minority – I do however applaud you and know that you will be able to overcome every hurdle thrown at you with the dogs you are training. I'm a firm believer that 99% of all dogs can be trained, given enough attention, time and patience. Most shelters are not in the position to give dogs this time, attention and patience, primarily because of lack of funds and since they are dealing with dogs that were already given-up on by someone else. The reality is that training a dog in a shelter is one of the worst environments for them. It's like setting up a MASH unit – you're going to do the best you can and that's as good as it's going to get.

Shelter dog training involves doing the very best you can do, and this book is not so much about the finer points of training – it is about getting a dog trained enough to get him adopted and saving his life. Having trained dogs of every temperament – from formal obedience to solving strong aggression – gives me the unique position to understand that shelter dog training is about saving lives, not winning contests for a perfect performance. It is also about using any tool we have in order to get the dog to a place where he can be saved and placed into a rescue or forever home.

Everything we do with a dog when it comes to training is geared toward the individual dog. We approach each dog as an individual. I do consider myself a motivational-based trainer and use primarily reward-based training. But I understand there are certain situations in which reward-based training will not work – these are the rarest exceptions, but they do exist. I WILL NOT give up on a dog if a particular training style doesn't work; instead I move to what will work.

I've been able to save several dogs by using motivational-based training when compulsion- or correction-based training didn't work. Yes, I said that right. There are dogs that will not train through compulsion that *will* train through motivation – just as there are dogs that will train through compulsion and not through motivation. The key is in understanding what training should be placed on what dog. This is something that can only be understood through years of training and understanding the temperament of dogs. It is not a judgment-call to be made by someone who disagrees with a particular style of training.

Training shelter dogs needs to be done by what I call the 80/20 rule. That is 80% success is enough, and striving for the other 20% to make the dog *perfect* is generally not an option. Most of the time, it would take another 80% effort to push for the other 20% of perfection – and that is not necessary and usually not an option. In other words, if we tell a dog to SIT and he sits crooked, that's fine. If the dog is sitting and we tell him to STAY, that is fine. Most competitive training doesn't allow for a STAY command after a SIT or DOWN command. We aren't worried about the details. Simply put, we want dogs that are obedient, not aggressive, and that will fit into a normal life. Dogs that are learning how to learn will make great candidates for adoption, and if the people want to continue training, more power to them.

We must also understand that training has to move along. If the dog doesn't respond to a toy or treats, we may resort to praise or a certain amount of corrections. It is our goal to save a dog's life. I am not saying that we need to –nor should we ever consider hitting a dog to get him to comply – but I am saying that a slight leash correction to get compliance is not out of the question. For those who oppose using corrections when other options fail, I'm certain that any shelter in any city will be happy to give you their dogs to train. You will be able to spend that *extra time* (the time shelters don't have) in order to move them along in a less compulsive way of training when nothing else works.

Knowledgeable people should handle training, and these people should possess good dog handing skills. They don't necessarily need to be accredited to be good; I know plenty of accredited trainers who suck and many non-accredited trainers that rock. If a person is good with dogs and can get a dog to progress in training, they're a good person to train a dog. People who get frustrated too easily, or those who think with their egos, should stay away from training dogs altogether.

The basics we need shelter dogs to understand are:
- Manners toward people and other dogs
- Engaging with people
- Basic obedience, including sit, down, come and walk on loose leash

Some people like to teach stay, but that is asking a lot of a shelter dog because there are so many variables in the STAY command. Basically, if I can get a dog to sit and not move when I take a step or two away, I'm happy with that. Anything else is a bonus.

Shelter dogs are training in a highly stressful environment, even if the training area is removed from the shelter itself. Remember, dogs digest their training after they return to their kennels. If those kennels are in the shelter, they will digest the training with some stress.

The key we want to focus on in our training is engagement with the human handler and teaching the dog to learn. Building this engagement is the key to moving the dog along the road to his forever home. Dogs that enjoy learning because they have been taught through a fair system will function well in homes. In the purest sense, we are *re-socializing* dogs and *re-teaching* them the skills they need to stay alive.

Reward-Based vs. Compulsion-Based Training

There are two basic types of training: ***Reward-Based*** and ***Compulsion- Based***. Used correctly, both are valuable. Used incorrectly, neither works and can be very destructive on the mind of the dog.

Reward-based training is more useful for most dogs, as it sets a fair and level playing field. The basic concept to reward-based training is, *"You do what I want you to do and I'll give you a reward."* That is a great philosophy and one that works as long as you have something the dog wants. And since most dogs want food, treat-training works wonders. This method can also be applied using toys as rewards toys.

Compulsion-based training differs, in that it uses a physical manipulation to *make* the dog do what we want him to do. Moving the dog physically into the movement we want isn't necessarily wrong, but it doesn't give the dog the opportunity to figure out what we want him to do by himself– we are *making* him do it. Dogs that learn through compulsion-based training often have a different relationship with their humans than those trained through reward-based training. Basically it is considered a more progressive way of learning when dogs can figure out what brings them reward and then do *that*. Happy-acting dogs complying with commands are often those trained through reward-based training.

Using a reward item, be it a toy or a treat, allows us to *lure* a dog into the position we are seeking. For example: using a treat to get a dog to follow along next to us for a few steps will create a different personality in a dog than if we yank his leash to gain compliance. This can most often be seen in the "*way in which*" a dog performs the task. Reward-based training, done properly, allows a dog to figure out what we want and he will gain his reward through doing it. Compulsion-based training forces him to do what we want and he gains reward by doing *it.*

A dog that is lured into creating a behavior will do so more willingly than one that has been physically manipulated to do so. This is mainly because he is able to perform the task and gain his reward – the quicker he performs the task, the quicker he gets his reward. The dog that is physically manipulated performs the task quicker only to avoid our correction.

It is worth the extra effort to shape a dog's behavior by luring him into the actions we are trying to teach, including sit, stand, stay, down, heel and come. Once we are clear the dog understands what we are asking, we have the option to correct his behavior if he *chooses* not to comply.

To teach a dog to sit using compulsion-based training, we pull up on his collar and push down on his butt as we say SIT. Yes, it teaches to dog to sit, but it also (if done too firmly) creates an opposition reflex in the dog. That is, the dog hears the word SIT and knows that a yank is coming on the collar and a push on his butt and anticipates that. He will respond with some aversion.

The flaw with both types of training is that dogs are either nagged or physically corrected too much because they are unclear as to what we want them to do. In order to teach more fairly, we want to use food to shape behaviors or lure the dog into the behavior we are asking and then reward either with food, toy or praise.

A great example is teaching a dog to sit with a treat:

We hold a small treat over the dog's head, and as he rocks back into a sit we reward him with the treat. We mark the behavior with a word such as YES and give him the treat. This should be repeated a few times during each training session. We can gently help the dog along by holding the treat above his nose (but not high enough to make him jump) and, if needed, tapping on his butt. The key is to keep the dog from being spooked and therefore trying to avoid our hand.

To teach down:

We show the dog a treat in our hand and place this (now closed) hand between the front paws of a (standing) dog. As he crouches down to get it, he will fold into a down and we reward him with the treat and the verbal marker YES. If necessary, because some dogs default to a bow (keeping the butt up), we may need to help them down by gently pushing on the shoulders toward the butt, to ease them into the DOWN.

Many reward-based trainers end up over-using the reward and *nag* the dog into compliance – and some never gain the compliance, which leaves both the dog and human frustrated. There is a time to use rewards and a time to use physical manipulation in training. The key lies in understanding what method to use and when. To put it simply: we use food to shape the behavior and get the dog to do what we want him to do. Then we slowly fade the food and continue to ask for the behavior and slowly introduce the physical assistance to help the dog along.

Using only one method of training or using the wrong method of training for the wrong situation is cruel to the mental clarity of the dog. There are countless dogs who suffer at the hands of trainers who confuse them to such a degree by their thick-headed, single-minded way of training.

In order to better understand true punishment, we can look at the training of positive-based training vs. compulsion-based training in the following ways:

With positive-based reinforcement, we show the dog a reward and withhold that reward until he figures out what we want him to do. Once he does it, we give him the reward. This is also referred to as *negative punishment* in that we withhold the reward until we receive compliance.

With compulsion-based training, we physically move the dog into the position we want him, and then reward him. This is also called *positive punishment* in that we correct the dog into the behavior that will bring him reward.

Although this description is very rudimentary, it is the basis of the two most common training methods currently used. It is my goal to open your mind to the most compassionate training by combining the two systems and giving the greatest chance to the most dogs.

Once dogs are clear and understand what we want, we can gain more excitable responses by substituting a toy as a reward item instead of food. I use food to teach behaviors and shape them, then switch to toys to gain more drive. It is my goal to get a dog to perform a task as quickly and energetically as possible: this is only possible through the use of an item that makes the dog truly excited – generally a toy.

There are some dogs that do not respond to food as a reward but will respond to a toy. It is the trainer's job to figure out what brings the dog to motivation and then using that tool, whether that is food or toys.

Under certain, but very limited situations, we will find dogs that do not comply with reward-based training. Certain dogs – those that are very high-drive or stubborn –may ignore food and toys and not comply with our training. If these dogs are simply aloof and low to mid-level drive, there is no need to force training upon them. However if they exhibit behaviors that make them unadoptable, we need to examine our options. Given enough time, almost every dog can be made to comply using positive-reward training. However, for those shelters that do not have the time and resources available to work with these dogs, there is a choice to be made. In the ideal scenario, it will be best to send these dogs to rescues that can spend the time and resources to help them. If this is not an option, using some compulsion in training at the shelter should be an option that should be considered before death.

For those who feel that there is only the *positive approach* and no other option, I find you as wrong as the people who feel there is only *compulsion* and no other option. Given that there *is* an option, it should be exercised if your goal is to save the lives of as many dogs as possible. Using corrections in training is not a mean method of training. Using pinch collars, choke chains and remote collars properly is not cruel, mean, wrong, or any other emotion you choose to attach to it. Using a tool properly is the key. We have domesticated dogs for thousands of years; it is our responsibility to give these animals any option available to save their lives.

Teaching the Basics

People look for some basic things when they evaluate a dog that they wish to adopt. These are the dog's overall personality, the way he interacts with people and his ability to do some basic commands. These commands include: sit, down, come and stay. They are relatively simple to teach to a dog and I will give you two methods to teach each one. The second method (compulsion) should only be used if a dog doesn't respond to the first (motivational).

***

DOWN: I prefer to teach a dog the DOWN command from a standing position. In the shelter environment, it is not that crucial but I will teach you the preferred method first. Because a dog will crawl forward into a down if he is sitting, teaching him from a stand will make the DOWN movement a much more natural technique for him, as he will rock backwards into it. This is why I am going to explain the DOWN command and ask you to teach it before the SIT.

__Method 1__: While the dog is standing in front of you, place a treat in your hand (closed fist) and place this hand between the dog's front paws. It's crucial that your closed hand lands between his front paws. This forces the dog to bend backwards and into the DOWN. Otherwise he will crawl forward continuously to get to the treat. It's important thing to keep your hand (holding the treat) still. The dog will try to figure out what he needs to do to get the reward. If your hand is moving, he will begin to follow the hand (and that is not what we want). Our goal is to have our hand remain still between his paws. As his head begins to move downward toward our hand, his shoulders will begin to rock backwards. At this point he can almost reach the treat, so to help him along we can push his shoulders down and back; that is *to push his shoulders toward his butt*. Here we say DOWN and, as his butt hits the ground, we say YES and open our hand to release the treat. Generally it only takes a few times of pushing/helping the dog's shoulders to get him to understand what we expect when we say DOWN.

* I urge you to be patient in teaching the DOWN command with the exercise above before progressing to Method 2.

Method 2: With the dog *sitting* next to you, keep one hand firmly on his leash or collar and with your other hand sweep his front feet out and forward. Push gently down on his shoulders to guide him into the DOWN. As soon as his belly touches the ground, reward him. This technique works best with smaller dogs. It's important to exude calmness when doing this so that the dog learns to stay in a down for a brief moment (that will increase with time). If we get too stubborn in forcing the dog into the down, the dog will see it as a fight and rebel.

Another method people use is to yank down on the dog's collar forcing him to the ground. I find this to be the least favorable method because it creates an aversion to the leash (which the dog sees as forcing him to the ground) as well as to the human at the end of the leash. In fact, I suggest *not* teaching the DOWN instead of teaching it in this manner. Eventually the dog will become compliant with other obedience techniques and will go to a down naturally. When he lays down on his own, it's a good time to "mark" the behavior and reward. I think it is the cruelest of techniques to crank a dog into a DOWN by placing undue leash and collar pressure on him. I've seen countless dogs learn the DOWN without ever using this technique.

If the dog is having hard time learning the DOWN, move to the next exercise and revisit this exercise later. Perhaps building some relationship into other techniques will resolve his compliance to the command he is finding difficult.

***

SIT: Sitting is something that dogs will do if they are paying enough attention to you and waiting for you to do something. The best possible scenario to teaching a behavior to a dog is to wait for the dog to do *that* behavior and then naming and rewarding it. For example, if the dog walks up to you, looks at you and sits, you can say SIT and give him a treat. The next time, try to say SIT *as* he is "sitting down" and when his butt hits the ground say YES and give him the treat.

Method 1: For most dogs, you'll simply need to hold the treat over their nose just high enough to make them rock back into a sit. As they rock into the sit, say SIT and when their butt hits the ground mark the behavior with YES and give them the treat. This is the method that will work with almost every dog.

Method 2: Some dogs may not be as food motivated or may just learn a little slower than others. For these dogs, we want to use a little compulsion to move them into the position so that we can reward them. With one hand on the dog's collar or slip-lead, place your other hand on his hindquarter and simultaneously push down on his butt as you slightly lift up on the collar. This will biomechanically move the dog into the sit position. When his butt hits the ground, say SIT, and reward him with praise and a treat, if he will take it. If he doesn't take the treat, make sure your praise is valuable enough to show your excited approval. Repeat this a few times, then remove your hands to see if the dog will do it on his own. Our goal in using this method is to teach the dog the biomechanics of the movement so he can do it on his own. We do not want to force the dog to sit, but instead we want him to learn what _SIT_ means.

***

COME: Teaching COME is as simple as rewarding the dog for being near you and, in my opinion, is one of the easiest things to teach a dog that has even the slightest bond with you.

During all phases of training, we have the dog dragging a leash or long line, and we begin teaching the dog this exercise at a distance no greater than the length of that line. In fact, teach the COME command from a distance of only a few feet to begin with.

Method 1: Standing at a distance of about 2-3 feet, show the dog a treat and move backward. As the dog begins to move toward you, say COME and take another step or two. When the dog gets to you, give him the treat and immediately repeat the exercise. The COME should be a very excited and positive engagement exercise. If the dog drifts off and wanders, we can step on the line and as the dog reaches the end and looks at us, we again say COME and encourage him to move toward us.

Method 2: For dogs that refuse to COME through motivational methods, we can use a more compulsive technique. Again, I encourage you to exhaust method #1 before you delve into Method 2. For this method we have a line attached to the dog's collar. We walk backward, away from the dog, and give a few slight pops on the line while saying COME.

**It's important to use several slight "pops" on the line, not one crushing blow. The hard yank will not encourage the dog to COME, but will instead encourage him to shut down and stop.

As we move backward while *popping* the line, the dog will move slightly toward us, and we need to encourage him in our tone of voice and demeanor. Getting excited will show the dog that his behavior is what we are asking for. We continue to *pop* the line and repeat the command. The dog will learn that the COME command is one he should do with excitement and happiness. We NEVER hit the dog or yank him in an aggressive way toward us. That only teaches the dog that being near us is a place of pain. The closer the dog gets to us, the more we turn off the compulsion. We only use the pressure as a last resort to get him close to us.

***

STAY: Since most of our focus is and always will be teaching our dog to be near us, STAY becomes a little confusing for some dogs. Here we are asking our dogs to *not do* what we've been teaching them in the past and *not do* what should seem natural for them, which is to follow us or be near us.

There really is only one way to teach the STAY command and that is by enforcing the STAY. For the record, a dog shouldn't necessarily need to be taught STAY after we give him a SIT or DOWN command because it's impossible for the dog to move away from the position while he is SITTING or DOWNING. This is a matter of principle, but I will teach you how to teach the STAY command here.

With our dog in a SIT (and that is probably the easiest to teach the STAY from), place your hand in front of the dog's face and say STAY. Move one step backward (while holding his line) and immediately return to the dog and reward him with a treat. Then release him by saying OK or FREE. Be careful not to put any tension on the line when initially moving backwards as this will confuse him into following you. Starting off at a short distance gives the dog a fair chance at learning and gives us a simple way to correct the dog if he makes a mistake. If the dog *breaks* the stay, don't yell or get excited. Simply say NO and move him back to exactly where you told him to STAY and repeat STAY.

Most dogs can only handle a very short distance on the STAY and need the distance built up over time. The key thing is not to have the dog STAY in the new place, but rather in the *first* place we asked him to STAY. If you allow your dog to move to another position and then ask him to STAY there, you are creating a game in your dog's mind. STAY means STAY and if he moves from that place he will be brought back to start the exercise again.

The key thing to remember in teaching STAY is to never reward your dog *before* you move away. It's common for the trainer to say SIT (then give the reward), then say STAY and move away. Since the dog was given the treat, he feels like he's been released and it's okay to move. When we add STAY to the SIT or DOWN command, we are stringing these commands together into one longer command and we can only reward the command when it has been completed.

Therefore, only give the reward when the exercise has been completed.

A fun exercise is to get the dog into a standing position and run him through all three movements: DOWN – STAND – SIT. Using a treat and the words together you can go from DOWN to STAND to SIT and back to STAND to DOWN. The key things to remember if you want to do this exercise properly is don't go from SIT to DOWN, simply follow this sequence:

STAND
DOWN
STAND
SIT
STAND
DOWN... then repeat.

This is a fun game and one that teaches good movement. It is also a good way to get a dog to understand the biomechanics of the exercises.

Walking on a Loose Leash

Everyone wants their dog to walk on a loose leash, but few dogs do so naturally and very few people ever do the work to get their dogs to learn this behavior. The reason most dogs don't learn to walk on a loose leash is because they gain their reward through the tension in the line. Teaching a dog to walk on a loose leash involves teaching him to gain his reward when he does the right thing: *respecting the slack in the line.*

To teach loose-leash walking, we first want to have a basic engagement with the dog. This can be done by spending a few moments with him before we start the walk. We want the dog to understand that the exercise is not an independent one, but one that we do as a team. His focus should be on you, not on where he decides. There are two ways to teach a dog loose-leash walking. Sometimes both methods need to be used as a continuum of force.

Method 1: With the dog on a slip-lead, position him to stand next to you on your left side. While there, take a piece of treat and give it to him from your left hip. Hold your hand at your hip and allow him to nibble. If he is a small dog or a puppy, you may need to bend down. The reason for rewarding him in this position is because we want him to see that *position* as the place he should be during the walk. If you give him the treat anywhere else, he will mark *that* position.

If the dog is food motivated, use something like string cheese or a hot dog in your left hand. Hold it there while walking and allow him to nibble on it while he's walking next to you. You can say HEEL if you like to teach him this position. This is not a formal HEEL, but for the sake of teaching our dog some basic manners it's all we will expect of him. The primary focus of this lesson is teaching the dog not to pull on the line and not to walk at the end of the line, choking himself. We want to allow the dog some freedom to sniff and potty, but we don't want him to start to drag us down the street. If we begin to allow this, it will only fester in the dog's mind and get worse. We want to stop this behavior quickly and fairly to the dog. If the dog is very high-energy and the reward at the side of the body doesn't work, we can simply follow Method 2.

Method 2: Again, using a slip-lead (or a choke-type collar with a leash attached), we use a double-belly system in our leash. This means that we have a slack of line that the dog is unaware of. Hold the leash in your right hand firmly, have a small (2-foot) slack of leash in front of you, and hold the line near the dog with your left hand. When the dog begins to pull on his leash, let go of the line with your left hand and maintain a firm grip with your right hand. Immediately turn 180 degrees. As the slack from the line picks up, _it_ will correct the dog back into position. The benefit to this system is that when the dog receives his correction, we are already going the other way. This teaches the dog that not paying attention gets him corrected. There is no guiding the dog here; it is simply a turn that allows the dog to correct himself through momentum.

The longer the line is, and the longer the duration from the time we turn to the time the dog receives the correction, the firmer the correction is on the dog. I generally opt to start with a 6-foot leash, as that seems to be the ideal for most medium-size dogs.

The benefit to this training is that, done correctly, the dog doesn't see the correction as coming from you, but rather from not paying attention. If you *guide* the dog along by keeping tension in the line, he will see you as *guiding* him along. He will rely on this for the rest of the walk. We want the dog to have some independence, but we require him to stay close and *check in* with us every once in a while.

**This method is not advised for older dogs, dogs with neck injury or very small dogs.

Excessive sniffing: Some dogs will use the "*I gotta go pee and pee and sniff and sniff*" technique in order to be crazy and erratic on a leash. If you allow this to continue, it will get to a point where the dog needs to mark on everything he sees. I try to avoid this in a very firm but fair way. I understand that the dog needs to relieve himself on a walk, but I always say, "*It's a walk – not an exploration.*" So, if a dog has this tendency, there is a simple solution. When I begin to walk the dog, I allow him to relieve himself. After he does, I give him praise or a reward and then begin a brisk and determined walk – one on which we will not stop no matter what. I might do this for 100 – 200 paces, then I stop again and allow him to potty, and again I give him a reward and praise. Then I repeat the determined walk for a bit longer, and give him another chance to relieve himself. It is best to do this several times, but *you* determine where and when he'll stop. This way he does get to relieve himself, but he is looking to you for the direction of where and when. We want the dog to learn that he should look to you even when it's time to potty.

What this teaches the dog is that he needs to "relieve himself" when he goes potty, but he should not mark everywhere. Once a dog begins marking, it is difficult to break him of this behavior because he becomes mentally obsessive. It's best to give the dog the tools to learn what we expect of him. By continuing to walk past everything he wants to mark on we keep his focus on the walk and on us. We give him several opportunities, during the learning phase, to relieve himself. As we progress, we can give him less and less opportunities, thereby breaking the destructive pattern of marking. The dog will be much happier on a walk without the mental frustration of having to stop and mark on every stone, and we will enjoy the walk more with our dogs.

Continuum of Force

If we want to give dogs a fair chance at life, we may sometimes need to apply a training regimen that will give them a fair chance at a forever home. In order to do this fairly, we must understand a continuum of force. Beginning with too firm of a correction is as wrong as continuing with too soft of a correction when the previous series of corrections have failed.

My philosophy is to start with a toy and treats, and where it goes from there is up to the dog. If I can retrain the dog trough solely positive means, that is exactly what I will do. However, I will NEVER give up on a dog when the politically correct methods of behavior correction don't work. As far as a dog's life is concerned, those who give up because they are afraid of the backlash from those who do not understand are no more helpful than the people who gave up on them in the first place.

Most dogs will respond to mild distractions, such as toys, treats and gentle physical redirections. These dogs are easily focused back to a handler when they act out. They may see a dog and start to lunge, but producing their favorite toy or treat brings them right back to their human, and all is good. For those dogs that have a higher level of *drive* or aggression, we need to *step up the correction*. Our primary goal is to see if the dogs will actually learn from the correction or if they will merely stop for the moment.

Our goal is to get dogs to learn their lesson for good and thereby *learn* to be good dogs. Furthermore, we want this behavior to carry over to other people who will be handling them, hopefully their owners. The dog must understand that the results of his unacceptable actions are causing discomfort (or the correction). He must understand that these actions are unacceptable, regardless of who is at the other end of the leash. It's imperative that the dog learns clearly from a fair correction and that this learning carries over to his future owner.

* The following shows a progression of correction. None of this should be done before working on engaging the dog through use of food and toys as rewards.

1. Start by withholding the reward. Simply put, we show the dog a treat and ask him to do something (or not do something). If he complies –he gets the treat.

2. The next level of correction is a verbal correction, followed by a slight pop on the leash. We tell the dog NO and enforce it with a physical pop or pull on the leash. If the dog complies, we praise and then ask him to do it again. If he does so without the correction, we give him a treat.

3. Escalating up the correction ladder, if the previous steps are not having any effect,

we use a physical manipulation of the dog's position. If he's looking at the object he should avoid (for example another dog) and shows aggression, we turn firmly 180 degrees and he will follow. We then immediately return to the starting point. He is given another chance. If he complies at that point, he is given praise and a reward.

4. If the dog continues to launch at the object or dog and is showing clear signs of aggression, we will give a physical correction. Provided you understand the temperament of the dog and know whether or not he will redirect his aggression, you will make a choice between the following options. In an ideal situation, option A precedes option B.

   a. Using either the end of the leash or a soft piece of rubber, I will pop it across the dog's nose or head in order to redirect him back to me. The stunning sound of this produces a very sharp *startle* effect. I'd like to note that the item you use for this should be soft enough not to inflict any injury. It is merely meant to startle the dog. The litmus I use to see if the object is too hard is hitting myself with it first. It can be the end of the leash, a soft piece of leather or a soft rubber hose. (Do NOT use garden hoses, dishwasher or washing machine hoses. This will cause serious injury to the dog.) Bicycle tire inner tubes are often a viable option.

b. If you sense there is even a probability that the dog may redirect onto you when startled, do not use option A. The better option is to momentarily incapacitate the dog by lifting his front feet off the ground. The dog should be on a choke-type collar or a slip-lead. This will not work with a flat collar or martingale and it should NOT be done with a prong collar EVER. To do this, we lift the dog up by the leash that is attached to the choke collar or slip-lead. We hold the dog up for a moment until he calms. We do not lift up sharply and drop him right away; we wait for the dog to *calm down.* If the dog is struggling and you put him down, he will escalate the struggle and the drive will get worse. The idea is to incapacitate the dog long enough to *stop* his behavior. It is imperative when doing this NOT to yell at the dog or hit the dog or connect with him in any way. The only connection is the leash around his neck. The leash is what is correcting him; we merely lift and say NO.

* It is important to note the Continuum of Force provided is intended to save the dog's life. Some dogs have been so hardwired for aggression that

the first 3 steps will not work. If they do not, you have an option, and it is one you should weigh very carefully. You can stop at #3 and accept that you cannot help the dog any further and make the decision to put the dog down. This is what most people will do in the given situation. If you feel the dog can progress, but simply needs a stronger lesson, you can go to step 4.

This method is not intended to be used lightly and it is not in ANY way intended to be abusive to the dog. It does not involve beating dogs or yelling at them. There is no continued physical correction beyond the pop on the snout or lifting the dog's front legs off of the ground. This is not the old method of helicoptering a dog in which the handler would lift the dog completely off of the ground and swing him around – doing this constitutes animal abuse. Furthermore, the physical pop on the snout is only intended to be done once – and that is when the dog refuses to redirect. There are no "multiple pops." One correction, correctly delivered with the intention to redirect the dog into compliance and to learn that this is what we need to save his life.

Understanding Aggression

Dogs that exhibit severe aggression are on the short list for being killed in our nation's shelters. Most rescues want nothing to do with dogs that are aggressive and turn their backs on them. Rescues are inundated with so many dogs that they often can't risk an aggressive dog coming in and wreaking havoc on their other dogs. This is very understandable; however, with some understanding of aggression, we can also give a chance to some dogs that may deserve one.

Aggression is often hardwired into the brain of the dog through experience. This experience is often built up over repeated experiences that went uncorrected.

If a dog barks at someone and they go away, the dog learns a lesson that "I bark, you go away." Later that behavior becomes ingrained in the dog's mind. Now the dog escalates the behavior: if the person comes close and he barks and you DON'T go away, he will bark louder and deeper. This barking will then progress to growling, snapping and eventually biting. If we catch the behavior early on, we can teach the dog that his barking is not necessary and that the person means no harm. This will negate his instinctual drive. We show him that the stranger means no harm and there's no need to take the behavior any further.

Dogs that are not socialized are not aware that strangers mean them no harm. They've probably had little, if any, social interaction to prove this. The same with children and dogs –we want to show a dog that children mean no harm and we try to give our dog many positive experiences around children. If in later years, they come across one child that does something foolish, the dog is more likely to forgive and NOT bite than the dog that is suspicious around children.

Aggression generally comes out of a dog's inner protective nature. This can be based on dominance or fear. The dog either wants to claim what isn't his (dominance) or is afraid to lose what *is* already his, including his safety (fear). We strive to understand what is driving the dog and deal with him in a fair manner. We want to show a dog that dominance has no place and will not be tolerated and we want to teach the other dogs that they have no reason to be fearful; irrelevant of past experiences, they are safe with us and anyone to whom we entrust them.

When aggression arises in a dog, whether it dominance or fear-based, a dog's inner drive takes over and his logical brain shuts down. Very similar to a case where a human is drowning, there is no sense of logic. There are many stories of a person trying to save a drowning victim, only to be physically injured by the flailing arms of the victim. Similarly, there are stories of dogs biting their owners in the throes of aggression that would never think of biting their humans in any other situation (even if provoked). The key thing to understand with aggression is that it "short wires" the brain into an *illogical shut down mode.* When the dog is in this state, no logic will redirect him; neither will treats, clickers or toys.

Dogs that can simply be redirected from aggression by a poke or a treat are generally not in the serious throes of aggression, but merely in a frustrated state. Understanding the difference between frustration and aggression will help us to better handle the dogs in our care.

If we can retrain a dog to avoid aggression by using a softer approach, it should be our primary focus. It should never be the goal of our behavior modification to employ strong physical corrections if they can be avoided in any way. Physical correction when dealing with aggression should be seen as the last resort in saving the dog from causing damage to someone else or himself.

When we open our minds to understand the strong physical drive of a dog in his *aggression mode* we should also open our consciousness to give the dog the tools he needs to stay alive in this world. Dogs that display aggression are a serious liability to everyone and cannot be placed into family homes; often their only option is a sanctuary or death.

Aggression is so often overlooked in its developing phase. People see some of the indicators but do nothing to stop it. This is often the case with puppies and young dogs. People think that the behavior will *fix itself* or the dog is just going through a phase. Countless cases that I have worked with can be traced back to owners who didn't know what aggression looked like, or they saw it but didn't want to do anything at the time to fix it. The problem is, the more aggression is left unchecked, the harder it becomes to eventually correct.

Dealing with the aggression drive of a dog requires us to understand that this drive reverts the animal back to his primal state. Take, for example, the situation of trained tigers turning on their owners and mauling them; these animals were trained and domesticated through selective breeding and – although not domesticated to the same degree as our family dog – were domesticated nonetheless. The inner drive of an animal is still there, and when it comes to *kill or be killed*, even a mouse will bite.

Because dogs, for the most part, still understand a hierarchical structure, they can often be rehabilitated by making the pack order very clear to them. This *rehabilitation* means getting the dog to *rethink* what he believes, to let go of the beliefs that he holds to be true.

To be very fair to the dog (which should remain our primary focus) we must give him the structure he needs to understand two things:

1. We mean him no harm and we won't put him in a situation that will harm him.

2. We will not allow him to act in a manner that will cause others harm (and thereby cause him the greatest harm).

To do this, we may have to put aside our mindset of political correctness and allow a dog to be a dog. We must treat him like a dog and give him the skill set to function in our human world.

Aggression is a very serious behavior and one that (left unchecked) is a death sentence for dogs. Society doesn't want aggressive dogs and neither do good family homes. If we don't want to correct aggression early on or fix it once it has developed we are saying it is okay. And by saying it is okay, we sentence the dog to death. Killing aggressive dogs has long been considered the best solution.

If we take the behaviors that start out as aggression and teach a dog to comply, our work will be a lot easier than having to face the monster head-on in later years.

It is important, as I mentioned previously, to be able to understand aggression and differentiate it from frustration or play. Dogs growl, bark and bite. Many times this has nothing to do with aggression – and yet people label dogs as aggressive that are not even slightly aggressive. Behaviors such as rough play, possessiveness and barking are seen as signs of aggression. Understanding the signs and utilizing the tools to help dogs through aggression is work that is best left to someone who understands this trait.

Aggression vs. Guarding

Although these two behaviors can be seen as similar, they have some inherent differences. The primary difference between aggression and guarding is that an aggressive dog displays aggression over various stimuli and *remains* aggressive after the stimuli are removed. Aggressive dogs may also be aggressive for the simple reason of *"just because."* A dog that exhibits *guarding* tendencies is one that acts aggressive in the vicinity of something he sees as his. This is often seen in food aggression, which is also grouped in with resource guarding. Food-aggressive dogs are often perfect dogs until you try to take their food or bones away from them – then you see their aggression drive come through. This aggression drive is solely limited to guarding things over which the dog is possessive – therefore he is exhibiting *guarding tendencies.* Differentiating between these two characteristics prevents us from "throwing the baby out with the bath water."

Truly aggressive dogs are a lot of work to retrain and there are those that can never be placed into normal family homes. However, It is our duty to differentiate behavioral issues and solve those that can be solved, while remaining realistic and not endangering a potential home with a truly dangerous dog. Food aggression and resource guarding (in their elementary phases) can be cured with a little bit of work. The next chapter shows the basic principles to retraining dogs with food aggression issues. Here I would like to deal with the difference between aggression and guarding.

Before we delve into the behaviors that can contribute to a dog being labeled as aggressive (and we begin training him or write him off altogether), we need to rule out any medical issues that could cause aggression due to pain. A basic blood panel and exam by a vet can rule out sprains, breaks, thyroid issues – as well as other medical issues that may cause a dog to act aggressively.

For a dog to be labeled as aggressive, he must display this *aggressive tendency* over various situations and after the stimuli has been removed, and he must be cleared of medical issues that would explain his personality.

Here's a short checklist:

- *Is the dog aggressive when someone walks by him? Does he follow the person once he passes by?*

- *Is he aggressive when someone pets him? If they stop petting, does he maintain his aggression?*

- *Is he aggressive when someone stares at him? Does he remain aggressive when they look away?*

- *Is he aggressive toward other dogs that are not bothering him? Will he lunge after a dog for no reason?*

- *Would he rather snap at a person than engage?*

- *When he hears a loud noise, does he go into aggression mode?*

If a dog shows intolerance to a majority of situations, perhaps he should be labeled as aggressive. However, if there only a few things bother the dog – for example, he snaps when we pull his tail – he shouldn't be labeled as aggressive. A simple note on his chart can suffice.

To give an example of this classification, let me tell you about a dog that showed some serious aggression when I temperament-tested him at a shelter. This dog was relatively calm in several aspects of the test, but when it came time to handling he flipped a switch. The first time I touched his tail he came after me with a vengeance (and I do say *touched his tail*, not *pulled on his tail*). It wasn't a snap; it was a full on attack. Because I had a good grip on the slip-lead holding him, I was able to control him and avoid a serious attack. I worked with him for a while and tried again. Again he attacked in such a way that would easily kill or maim a small child. This is what I considered a serious aggression streak that surrounded only one thing, his body. If he had been guarding, he would snap and that would be it. But continuing the attack was a sign of aggression. Due to the level of aggression and the fact that he would not regress when I stopped touching him, I considered him "aggressive."

If a dog is food-aggressive, he will snap when you come near his bowl, but when you stand still or move away he will go back to eating. Remember, the plastic hand test (one I'm not a big fan of) works mainly when the hand is moving. If I place the hand next to the bowl, the dog generally will growl and go on eating. It is only with repeated movement and interaction and nagging engagement that the dog will eventually attack the hand. It is this *pestering* of the dog that makes him act out.

One method for curing food aggression or resource aggression is to remain in the proximity of the object, and not move away or not move in to take the object. We thereby teach the dog that our presence does not mean we are there to interfere. If the dog is clear that nothing will change with our presence, he is likely to remain calm. With enough exposure to the presence of a neutral person, the dog has the opportunity to relearn his behaviors.

Another thing to watch for is how the dog handles your presence. Some dogs, may growl, but given the opportunity they will take the object and move away with it to another area of the room or yard. This just shows a possessive streak. I tend to retrain this with replacement objects. If a dog is possessive over the tennis ball, I'll offer him another ball to get *his* ball away from him. Please see the explanation below. It's a simple logic for the dog to begin to learn fairness: *If I give you this – I get that.* And remember, most dogs are like children – they always want what you have, not what they have.

When looking to classify a dog as aggressive instead of possessive, be certain to watch the dog's overall drive toward objects and the shift that may occur when the dog gets the object. It's important to see if their possessiveness incites possessive or aggressive behavior. The reason we want to watch this is that the training of these dogs should be geared toward the root of the issue, not the surrounding issues. For example, a dog that is possessive toward an object and displays aggressive tendencies when that object is around, should be taught that losing his aggression will bring him more reward than trying to keep the object all to himself. This can be done by playing some fair games with the dog.

If a dog is possessive over a toy, it may come from the learned behavior that when someone takes the toy, the game is over. If the dog thinks that every time I reach for his toy I'm going to take it away and playtime will stop, he may be correct in assuming a possessive tendency toward his toy. We must teach him that we will be fair in playing.

For example, we can teach a dog that is possessive over a tennis ball to lose this drive. We play a simple game with the dog called *two-ball:* we bring out the first tennis ball and ask the dog to perform a command – let's say SIT

173

The reason I always ask for a behavior such as SIT before I give a dog a reward is to put myself in the position of power and the ability to produce something he likes. This sets the stage for gaining obedience early on. The dog must see clearly that I control the game. If he doesn't do what I want him to do, I'm not going to start the game. This is a simple piece of logic but it goes very far in setting the stage in the dog's mind.

Once the dog sits, we reward him with a verbal cue, for example YES, and throw the ball. When he returns to us with the ball, we produce the other ball. We can animate the ball and make it more interesting. Once his focus shifts to the other ball, we wait for him to drop the ball in his mouth (or we may reach to take the ball). Then we immediately throw the ball in our hand. When he returns, we repeat the process with the original ball he left us. Once the dog catches on to this concept, the speed can be increased and the dog's enjoyment of the game takes over his possessive tendencies toward the ball. Eventually we can add in a command such as DROP and, as soon as the dog complies, we throw the other ball.

This *replacement* concept with two toys works best if we have two identical objects. Since most dogs are possessive over a toy, it's very worthwhile to have duplicate toys for behavior modification training. This logic does not apply to food dominance or aggression. Please see the separate chapter on this.

Solving Food Aggression

This is a slight modification of an online article I posted on my website some time ago. I am including it in this book because of the important information it contains. It can easily be modified to deal with food aggression at a shelter or rescue using dog-savvy volunteers. This information can also be passed along to adopters to prevent the return of dogs with food aggression issues.

Understanding why a dog has food aggression issues is the first step to potentially solving the problem in a fair manner.

To a dog, food is the ultimate resource – much like cash is to a human. If someone steals your money you can't buy anything. Conversely, dogs can't buy food, so if you take their food away, they're stuck. Some dogs (in particular ones that come from shelters) may have serious food aggression issues. This is because food is in short supply, and if they were kenneled with other dogs, they may have lost the battle for food. Since dogs need food to live, they will fight for it with their lives.

If a dog has food aggression issues, it is something you will want to address in a straightforward manner, and sooner rather than later. People make the ultimate mistake when they let food aggression go and think, "*It will work itself out.*" **It doesn't!** Once a dog has food aggression issues, it's a downward spiral unless you're willing to do the hard work to help your dog. If you give up on your dog, rest assured of one thing: no one else is going to be able to, or want to solve the issue. So, more than likely, giving up on him is signing his death certificate. He knows you, he trusts you, and we will use this relationship to our advantage and teach him that he doesn't need to be aggressive for food, or anything else for that matter.

Food aggression with dogs can be related to other dogs and to humans as well. If properly used, a few key strategies can help you resolve the overall concept in the dog's mind. Not all dogs have food aggression issues for the same reasons, and it is not something that is prevalent only to adult dogs. I've seen puppies as young as 8 weeks have food aggression. Although it is easier to solve at a young age, left unchecked, a dog with food aggression issues can develop into a monster.

Food Aggression Toward Humans:

In order to solve the mental confusion in the dog's mind we need to make two things very clear to him:

1. You have the food and you control the food.

2. As long as he's good, there will always be food.

It is not a good idea to try to handle food aggression by taking food away from a dog that is being aggressive. That is the old "Put the plastic hand in the bowl" method – and it is really stupid and unfair to a dog. The reason is because this logic is counterintuitive to the dog. It would better to *not give the dog the food in the first place.* If I put a food bowl down and reach for it and the dog snaps, and I then take the bowl away, the dog's action was justified. In the dog's mind, you were trying to take his food, he snapped to protect his food, and then you took it away, so he was right: *When someone reaches for the bowl, they really are trying to steal my food, so I should bite to protect my food.*

The dog must be clear that you control the food **before** you give it to him. In canine behavior the leader dog eats, and when he walks away, he rarely comes back and pushes the other dogs out of the way because *he wants more.* Using this logic, we will provide food to the dog in small increments, all the while creating a bond between the dog and us.

Dogs that have food aggression issues should be fed in a methodical way. The single best approach is to begin with a hand-feeding regimen. That is to say, everything the dog gets to eat comes from my hand. Let's break this down simply. The food is given to him in small amounts from my hand. The bowl is not near the dog – my hand is – and he only sees my hand as delivering the food. If he tries to circumvent my hand to go for the food, he doesn't get any. Don't correct the dog at this point. Simply move away and show him the food is in your hand. Reload your hand while he is chewing on the food you just gave him. Waiting until he's done chewing, then reloading, steers him toward the bowl or bag containing the food. We don't want that. His focus is to remain on you because your hand contains the food.

A professional should handle dogs that are so severely food aggressive that they will attack you to get to a bag of food or the bowl. In these cases, we often opt for feeding a dog through a crate or barrier. The techniques described here will address dogs that become aggressive when you reach for their food.

Do not do this exercise with other dogs around or other food bowls on the floor. It's just you and the dog and the food. This is called *learning without distractions*. Right now we need to be fair and clear to the dog. Feed him a few kibbles at a time or – if you're raw-feeding – a small amount of the raw food. This regimen takes time. *Take your time* and have patience. It is the patience that you exert that teaches him patience – and it also teaches him not to behave stupidly.

When offering the dog his food, be cautious not to jerk your hand away. Present your hand with the food in it, open your hand (palm up) and let him take the food from your hand. Then slowly and deliberately reload your hand. I try to make a habit of bringing my hand toward the dog. This further teaches him that we are delivering the food and he does not need to be aggressive to get it.

Once the dog begins taking the food from your hand for a few days, you can begin making him wait for the food and even begin dropping some food into a bowl beneath him. This action will teach him that your hand moving toward a food bowl is an action that delivers food, not a negative one that takes his food away. We want to teach our dogs that our hand moving toward a food bowl is a good thing.

Once the dog is clear that he is going to get fed, he should begin to lose some of his food aggression. Remember, he is protecting what he thinks is valuable. Once he figures out there is always more, it will lose its value and he will calm down. The other thing he will figure out is that *you* control it, not him. His deference to you will teach him structure as well.

I have faced this issue on several occasions, especially with raw food and raw bones. I have fixed this by holding raw bones for my dog while he chewed them. Once he had taken a few bites of meat off the bone, I placed the bone down and walked away. Over time he saw that my hand was no threat to him and he relinquished his position and aggression to the food. Now I have no issue taking raw bones out of his mouth. (I do not suggest you try this too soon and definitely not with a dog you do not know.)

Food Aggression toward Other Dogs:

Dogs that exhibit food aggression toward other dogs should be broken down into two categories:

1. Those that walk away from their bowls in order to steal another dog's food.
2. Those that become aggressive when another dog approaches their bowl.

Both are wrong, but the first is more wrong. Neither should be tolerated.

To begin with, dogs that show any food aggression toward other dogs should be taught that this behavior moves them to the bottom of the ladder and they are fed last. By seeing everyone else eating first, they learn that their place is not up for negotiation. When restricting the dog from eating, you'll need to keep him restrained so that he doesn't try to sneak in and get food from the others. This is easily done by keeping him on a leash while the others are eating. If he tries to pull toward them, tug on the leash and give him a calm NO.

When everyone else is finished, they should leave the room and you can put his bowl down and allow him to eat. Do not give up your position. You control him. Giving up and just saying "Whatever," may land you in a heap of trouble. His aggression will escalate. If you're certain that the other dogs present are well trained enough where they won't bother him, you can leave them in the room. I would also encourage you to make the dog sit and wait before allowing him to eat. This will teach him more about structure. I don't tolerate dogs that push over me to get to their food. One exercise I do with my dog is place the bowl down and then I leave the room. I expect my dog to wait until I give him the OK command to eat. Just because it goes down, doesn't mean it's his yet. In the same respect, once it is his, *it is his* and I don't act like a jerk and take it away. Because I am this fair with my dog, *if* I have to take it away, he's not going fight me for it.

Dogs that leave their bowl to go to another dog's bowl must be corrected immediately. When training for food issues, I suggest letting the dog drag a leash or a long line so that you can easily reach him without having to grab his collar (and inevitably get bit). As soon as the dog leaves his bowl and begins heading toward someone else's bowl, I give him a verbal NO. Assuming you've taught your dog the NO command, he should stop to look at you. When he does, you direct him back to his bowl, either with a signal or by use of his leash. If he insists on continuing, give him a physical correction on the leash following the verbal NO. If he still insists, remove him from the room, remove his food and he doesn't eat.

Remember, if he moves away from his bowl, he's done. He will learn that he must focus on his bowl and not someone else's bowl if he wants to eat in your house. At the next feeding he will have the opportunity to try again. After a few tries, even the toughest dogs will learn. Do not make the mistake of taking him to another room and feeding him. Provided your other dogs don't have food aggression issues, you can easily teach the *problem* dog with a small amount of work. If your other dog(s) have food issues too, you probably have not done the work in teaching structure to them. It is your job to protect your dogs, so do not subject a dog to getting bit by being sloppy. Corrections, whether physical or verbal, should be delivered calmly... that means *no screaming.*

Most dogs can be corrected or retrained with structured feedings. Some dogs require physical corrections – it will depend on the severity of the food aggression and how clearly you can teach him. I remind you that some of the most severe aggression a dog can exhibit is over food, so be careful. At the very first signs of food aggression, you must take control. Physical corrections should be done fairly and calmly, but instantly. As soon as the dog moves off of his bowl, he should be corrected. Once he approaches the other dog's bowl, it's too late. It is your job to keep him at his bowl. You are his leader - take this role seriously. And take it seriously because if you don't fix this, it is a death sentence for your dog. One of the hardest things to deal with is food aggression especially if it escalates to a place where two dogs are aggressive toward each other. *It never works its way out.* Catch it early and you'll fix it. Let it go and you'll lose a dog.

An important thing to remember is that the person who is doing this training should be a professional or the primary caregiver of the dog, never a housekeeper, child or stranger. This is about building upon a relationship with the dog, which makes the training fair.

Dogs that growl or snap when another dog approaches their bowls are not as wrong as the dog that purposely wanders over to another dog's bowl. These are the bullies. I suggest you teach your dog that his food bowl is his food bowl; he is not to approach another dog's food bowl while there is a dog eating out of it.

A dog protecting his food with a warning is acceptable, but not preferable. We will want to address this issue by teaching the wandering dog first, as instructed above. If another dog is simply walking by the bowl and the dog that is eating becomes perturbed, we will want to teach him two things: One is that we don't accept aggressive behavior for the sake of aggressive behavior. And, most importantly, because we are there to maintain order in the pack, we will not allow the other dog to take his food. Because of that, the dog is not allowed to growl at the other dog.

Using these techniques is generally enough to get most dogs into line to understand structure. I suggest that you be vigilant in the use of a long line or at least a leash on the dog you are training. When it comes time to correct the aggressor, do so in a fair but firm manner. The punishment must fit the crime. When it comes to aggression (and other methods don't work) I am in favor of physical corrections, simply because if you don't correct them for being aggressive to one another, they will try to sort it out themselves. That is the very worst thing that can happen. It is better that you sort it out for them – that is the job of the leader.

I do not advocate physical corrections for training dogs, but I do for combating aggression in these types of situations. I've dealt with hundreds of dogs with severe aggression issues and would caution you against allowing this behavior to continue after the first time you see it. Nipping it in the bud is not difficult if you catch it early on. Let it go and you've got a nightmare on your hands.

In my home there is no aggression toward food, toys, people, other dogs, places – nothing. I do not tolerate it. Yet I run my house in a very casual manner. My dogs are allowed on my furniture. They get lots of love and attention. They can basically do as they want as long as they understand that I control the house, and when I've had enough, it stops. We play and have a great time and there are no issues. All of this is a result of fair training and a good relationship with my dogs.

Dealing with Fear-based Aggression

A dog that exhibits fear-based aggression is very different to deal with than a dog that exhibits dominance-based aggression. Although some of the symptoms may look the same, we need to look at the causes before we look at the outward signs. Of course, our primary concern needs to be our safety, so please take extreme caution when dealing with any dog-training situation – especially those that include aggression.

One of the more common outward signs we see in dogs displaying fear-based aggression is a lunging, then an immediate regression. Another sign is a dog that that barks wildly while always regressing/moving backward. In fear-based aggression, the dog will often work himself into a position where he is forced to bite. He leaves himself no room for escape by constantly backing up, and if we're not aware of what we're doing, we may force him into a position where he will bite and he will fail.

Our goal is to put the dog into a position where he will NOT fail, even if we need to control the situation completely. When first approaching a dog that is fear-based, wait and observe the dog. See what triggers his fears and take them into consideration. These fears can be anything from the sex of a person, to the clothes they wear, to the way they approach the dog. The absolute wrong way to approach a fear-based dog is straight on. I suggest a mild sideways approach, never looking directly into the eyes of the dog. We don't want the dog to see us as a direct threat, and approaching sideways will lessen the impact of our presence.

Before attempting to leash the dog, it is best to spend some time in the dog's presence without doing much of anything – especially talking. One of the biggest mistakes I see trainers, shelter employees and volunteers make is vocalizing too much with the dog. Talking to a dog that is afraid or confused generally escalates the issue instead of solving it. This is even more pronounced when people talk in a very high-pitched tone. If you must talk, use a low, calm, quiet tone. To begin with, I'll often spend a few minutes just sitting outside of the dog's kennel (or even inside if he is okay with it). I will toss a few treats in his general direction. Bearing in mind that a highly stressed dog will not eat, you are tossing the treats out to show that you are there on fair terms. It is not your goal to get the dog to eat the treats, but instead you are showing the dog a sort of a *peace offering*.

While I'm near the dog, I watch his overall body language. Is he getting stiffer or beginning to relax in my presence? If he's starting to loosen up, I can move closer and introduce the leash. I do this by throwing it gently into his general direction and allowing him to sniff it, then reeling it back. By doing this, I can desensitize the dog to the presence of a leash. If time permits, I will leave the kennel altogether and return a few minutes later. The more time you can give a dog to desensitize toward that which brings him fear, the more fair your approach will be seen by the dog.

Our goal is not necessarily to wipe the fear out of the dog's mind, but instead to teach him that there is nothing to be afraid of in our presence. Since most dogs with fear-based aggression focus that aggression toward humans, we can be the catalyst to teaching them this valuable lesson.

In solving fear-based aggression, we allow the dog time to understand that what he is afraid of will bring him no harm. This is generally done through gradual desensitization. There are a host of things that the dog could be afraid of in a shelter environment, including the people, the environment, the kennel itself, the leash– as well as other dogs. These fears should subside with fair interaction with us. We want to build up the dog's confidence so that his fears will be diminished. Using too much pressure on the fear-based dog may or may not scare him into compliance, but it will never build his confidence enough to overcome his fears.

Once we spend enough time around the dog we can try to make some slight physical contact without putting too much pressure on him. Be aware that if a dog is cornered in his cell and you try to make contact, he may bite. A dog that has no room to escape is forced to do what he can to protect himself, so be aware of his surroundings before attempting contact. I've found that many dogs will initially run away when approached. I prefer to allow dogs to do this because it teaches them that *they have a way out.* As long as the dog feels that he can escape, he is less likely to bite. This will put him on a more rapid road to recovery.

The best option to helping the dog is to remove him from his environment, thereby giving him a new picture. To do this, we're going to need to leash him. Using a slip-lead will make this much easier. I can open the noose of the leash as wide as necessary and toss it over the dog's head. It may take a try or even a few to get the leash around the dog's neck. Remain patient. Remember not to stare the dog in the eyes and don't stand squared off in front of him. This could cause conflict in the dog's mind. When I say not to stare into the dog's eyes, I am not saying that you should not keep your eyes on the dog. It is paramount that you watch for signs in case the dog attacks. What I am saying is do not stare the dog DOWN. Watch him, see him and be aware.

Once the dog is leashed, it is best to quickly move him out of his kennel. Don't fidget with the dog or try to coax him along now that he is leashed. Simple say, "LET'S GO" and begin walking out of the kennel to a designated room or play yard. The fact that he is walking next to you is a key exercise in his mind and a great stride toward building trust and curing his fears. Do so fairly and in a determined manner. This is no time to overthink or coddle him. Just keep moving to your destination.

Once you arrive at your training area, try to slowly engage the dog by offering him treats or a touch on the head. Keep your interaction short and positive. If there are other people around, don't allow them to put the dog in a place where he feels too much pressure. This can include trying to touch him, offering him treats or toys or even speaking to him. Allow him to just hang out while you speak with others who are in the area. If he seems interested in them, they can offer him a treat.

The most important thing is for this interaction to be between you and the dog. Out in the training area, introduce other items such as toys, treats, chairs, etc. This should be a shared experience between you and the dog. Everything should remain positive. This is no time to begin introducing any training routine. Keep it light and keep it fun.

After a short while (10-20 minutes) return him back to his kennel. Walk him into his kennel, remove the leash and leave him a treat. Turn and walk away without too much interaction. It's important not to make a big deal about your leaving at this point. We want him to keep in his mind the positive interaction you shared. Later this will all happen again.

The more often the dog can experience this interaction, the better it is. It is very beneficial for the dog to have a couple of these experiences in one day if possible. The more often a positive imprint is repeated, the more quickly the negative imprint will be overcome.

When dealing with fear-aggression, it is important to build the dog up before introducing corrections or formal obedience. Allowing a dog the positive experiences through neutral interactions and building on those successes will imprint positively on his mind. This will bring him along much faster than giving an instruction such as a command, which may require a correction. Once the dog has some basic understanding of relating to a person or situation in a way that does not feel threatening, we can begin to introduce obedience training.

Dealing with Dominance-based Aggression

Dogs that exhibit dominance-based aggression are the smallest percentage of the aggression cases we see in shelters. Too often, *all aggression* is lumped into dominance-based aggression, or aggression is just seen as *aggression* without ever taking the time or effort to classify the difference(s). This is a big mistake and often causes unfair assessments to be placed upon dogs, thereby costing them their lives.

Before I speak too much about dominance-based aggression I want to clarify an important point: Just because a dog is dominant, does not mean he is aggressive. Some of the most stable dogs are dominant dogs. They have the confidence and stable temperament that is needed to deal with the stress of life and difficult training. Many dogs in dog sports, police work, narcotics and SAR, as well as protection work, are dominant dogs and it would be a big mistake to classify them as aggressive just because they are dominant.

Dominance-based aggression can be equated to a dog being a *bully* and doing everything *his* way. If you try to change his way, he's going to bite you. What we need to do with a dog that has serious dominance-based aggression is "put him in check." We need training and interaction to be fair and, most importantly, we need him to understand that we are in charge and he isn't. The old saying, "Give him and inch and he'll take a mile," couldn't be truer than with dominance-based aggression.

The very first thing we do with these dogs is to infuse structure, and that usually starts with food. I prefer to start training with hand feeding to show the dog that all good things will come from my hands, and if he pushes it, the correction will come from these same hands. He will do everything that I ask, and he won't do anything that I don't ask for. His world should revolve around my every word. He will be put in check to keep him safe and give him a life.

Over the years I've dealt with many dominantly aggressive dogs, and I attribute my success in dealing with them to the fact that I develop somewhat of a relationship with them *before* I begin training. This prevents having to over-correct them to assert my position. It's not difficult to walk into the kennel of an aggressive dog and whack it into compliance. In fact, if you don't get bitten (or torn apart), you end up with either of two situations: either the dog will comply to your will or you will push him into fear, and he will see the world through fearful eyes – he may then become a fear-aggressive dog. The primary concern should be to take the dog down a couple of notches to eliminate his aggression, but not to take the dog into a place of fear. Gaining compliance from a dog that is dominantly aggressive is a matter of mutual respect.

You will never coax these dogs from dominance into compliance; this compliance must be earned: by you! You need to show the dog that you are strong and fair and that you will demand and gain his respect.

I begin my interaction, as always, with food. I approach the kennel, stand somewhat sideways and wait. I don't confront him with a square body posture because I don't want him to think I'm there to confront him. I start out fairly – where it will go after that is up to him. If he wants to comply, we won't have any issues. I usually start by tossing some treats in front of him and slowly start to drop them closer and closer to me until he is close enough to take them from my hand. I watch his overall body language. If he takes the treats, we're halfway home. If he doesn't and lunges and barks, I can make one of two determinations: I can wait until he is hungry, and start hand-feeding him (which is my first choice), or I can get him leashed and deal with a little more compulsion. If you pull him through this difficult phase by luring him through hand feeding, you're much further ahead of the game. If hand feeding won't work or you just don't have the time, move ahead one step below.

It's important to understand that after *getting compliance* by the use of compulsion, you'll still have some training to do. If you can safely get a slip-line around the dog, do so by offering him some food and then putting the leash over his head. If this isn't an option, you can opt for using

193

a catchpole to keep the dog from attacking you. I generally don't condone the use of these poles, as they set a very negative imprint on the dog and that takes much work to undo, especially if you are the person placing the pole around his neck.

I've spent extended periods of time leashing dogs in order to avoid using catchpoles. If absolutely necessary, use as short a pole as is safely possible. Once the dog is on the pole, our goal is to get the dog into a compliant place so we can remove the pole and begin training.. To do this, keep the noose of the pole as loose as safely possible, and place a lead over the dog's head while he is still on the catchpole. This requires two people and I suggest discarding the catchpole once the slip-lead is in place. Be certain that the dog begins to settle allow him to see that there is no tolerance for his aggression. If the dog exhibits redirected or handler aggression, use precautions – including the use of two lines and two people.

I want to assure you that there are countless dogs that become very good dogs after just a short amount of time training. Understanding that shelters are stressed with time, staff and resources, I want to be sure that we give every dog a fair chance without placing staff members at any undue risk of injury. If a dog needs to be put down for aggression issues, we want to be clear that we have assessed them and at least tried to work with them. It is very clear to staff which dogs are hopeful and which ones aren't. We can't spend too much time trying to rehab every dog that is aggressive, but this section is dedicated to those worthy of the effort.

It's always been my position that given enough time and resources all but the very smallest percentage of dogs can be retrained and I've proven this in some of the toughest cases. Every dog that we can give a chance to is a victory to our mission of giving hope to the hopeless.

Once the dog is safely on the slip-lead, we can begin working with him. It will be crucial to determine where his aggression lies. I've seen many cases of dogs that had leash issues that I thought they would be a challenge, but they ended up being just perfect once the leash was safely around their necks. Others come to the shelter with collars that are so tight that they fight to the death when a hand comes near the collar. Once we remove these collars, the dog is fine. These are all things that I like to address when looking for the behaviors that trigger the initial aggression. The primary aggression I'm concerned with here will be handler-based aggression: that is aggression to the person on the other end of the leash. There are several types of aggression that we look for, including:

Aggression when handled - This refers to dogs that don't like to be touched and will bite or attack when we try to handle them.

Aggression when corrected on leash - These dogs will turn and bite whoever is on the other side of the leash when we give a sharp leash correction.

Redirected aggression – This is mainly the case of dogs that display aggression to other dogs or people, and when we try to correct them or get near them they "re-direct" their aggression toward us.

Unprovoked aggression – This is the worst one, and the most dangerous, because the dog will just bite for no real reason, and usually without any warning signs.

Environmentally influenced aggression – These are dogs that are "spooked" by anything, be it a sound or the sight of something, and then flip into aggression.

In all of these cases, it is important to remain neutral toward the dog's behavior. The reason this is so crucial is that excitability generally causes the dog's drive (be it aggression or fear) to escalate. If we need to deliver a correction, it should be done firmly and fairly, and without any emotion from us.

In order to protect the handler, I often use a double-noose system. . The importance of protecting the staff and volunteers is paramount; these dogs should only be handled by dog-savvy people who have the physical ability to control the dog they are dealing with.

Using the "double-noose" system entails using two slip-leads, held by two different people, each standing parallel to the dog. There should be no tension on the lines, but they should not be loose either. At this point, either person can move toward the dog and begin handling (or a third person can do it). If the dog makes a move toward the person handling, the backup person has a line to control the dog. The critical thing is that – no matter what – neither person lets go of their line. This will keep the dog safely tethered between the two lines. . I've had someone at the other end of a double-lined dog panic when the dog turned toward them. They dropped their line and the dog came after me. As long as both people are holding onto their line, there is a relative amount of security.

Once we determine the dog's level of aggression, and what triggers the aggression, we can work with one line and maintain control of the dog. The key is to determine the level of aggression and what it will take to stop it. Some dogs can be corrected with a "pop" on the leash and they will stop their behavior – others need a lot more. Figuring this out will allow us to determine if a dog can be rehabilitated and safely adopted.

We want to make humane decisions for dogs, as well as for the community, and adopting out a dog that has severe aggression issues does no good for dog or human. Our goal is to determine if we can change the mindset of the dog into an adoptable pet. We want the dog to see that we aren't challenging him and furthermore that he should not challenge us – and if he does challenge us, he's not going to win. Every dog I've ever worked with accepted the fact that if he can't win, he'll comply – this is just the way it is in the dog world (unless the dog has a medical impairment).

I've seen a good friend and dog trainer take a police dog gone-bad and retrain him in a few weeks into a very nice dog. It's just a matter of time and dedication.

If a dog begins to challenge us, we want to interrupt his behavior or "block" his aggression. I do this by simply *disabling* his attack through lifting his front feet off of the ground by use of the slip around his neck. This is not *helicoptering* a dog and swinging him around with all four legs off of the ground; it is simply lifting up on the line and *disabling* his attack. This takes enough air and power away from the dog to allow him to *settle* back and think about his actions. We want to calm him and put him back to a place where we can start again. This is meant for only the toughest of candidates and it is also the toughest of techniques – it should only be done by someone who understands the technique. This should only be done when other methods fail. Placing a dog into a situation where we immediately need to correct him is not fair to the dog and not safe for us.

The reason this works better than a physical correction such as a pop to the snout is because it creates no challenge or confusion in the dog's mind. The dog is challenging us directly and he will see that his challenge is unfounded. I've used this technique in dealing with various aggressions – including dog-to-dog aggression – with great success. I stress that it is the very last step in training before the needle in the back room. We try to exhaust every other technique and use this as our final option when nothing else works.

For years, police departments used chokeholds to subdue assailants and all but a very few lived to be tried in court. Here we have a similar situation, and we clearly know for certain that the dogs that are this aggressive will 100% be killed in the back room if we can't help them through training. So in temporarily disabling the dog, we protect the human and give a chance to the dog we are working with.

When the dog triggers, we use a verbal cue "NO" and lift the dog straight up. There is no jerking motion, simply UP. The person doing this should have the physical (and mental) strength to lift the dog and hold him there until he calms. The key part to disabling him is to hold him there until he calms. It is a big mistake to let the dog down too soon; this will only incite more aggravation – and exacerbate the problem. No matter how irate the dog becomes, he will calm down, given the time. I've seen dogs pass out from lack of air using this technique and recover just fine afterwards. As long as the dog is healthy and is lifted up (and not jerked abruptly), the technique works in most all cases. Older dogs and dogs with neck and throat issues are generally not good candidates for this technique and are often the ones we need to put down for their behavior without trying to rehabilitate them.

Disabling in this manner is not the most politically correct thing for the uneducated public to see, but it is a technique that we should opt for as a last option before killing the dog for something that could possibly be corrected. For those that criticize these techniques, I can tell you that there are countless dogs that are alive today because trainers didn't listen to criticism and instead opted to give dogs a chance. If you choose to be one of these people, you'll undoubtedly be criticized, but you should know that those you are trying to save have no other hope.

Once the dog recovers from the correction, he will generally respond in a meeker manner and can then be given praise and positive attention. We want to mark the good behavior so that the dog understands, or at least learns to understand, the behavior we are aiming for. The dog should be given the chance to succeed in as many ways as possible, and this should involve re-introduction to the stimuli that caused him aggression in the first place. When the stimulus is re-introduced, and if the dog shows no aggression, we want to mark that moment in time and then praise and reward. The more often the dog receives the rewards, the faster he should learn to understand that his bad behavior has no place. Our goal is to block the bad behavior as quickly and completely as possible so as to cause the dog the least amount of confusion.

Understanding that we have a very short amount of time in the shelter environment puts us in the unique position to help as many pets as possible in the shortest amount of time. Each life we can rehab and adopt out gives us the opportunity to save another. As is the case with aggression, the faster we can solve the problem in the dog's mind, and the clearer that lesson is to the dog, the better we are performing our duties.

The Feral Dog Dilemma in Shelters

Feral dogs are those dogs that were once domesticated and have reverted to a wild state. Although many dogs are classified by shelters as being feral, very few of these dogs are *truly* feral.

Truly feral dogs lack all of the social skills of domestic dogs and are generally at least a second-generation wild or feral offspring. The dog that has simply been living on the streets as a result of abandonment may exhibit feral qualities but lacks the core feral state. Since these dogs once enjoyed socialization with humans, they are merely shifting to a wilder state or *survival mode*. There is much evidence to prove that these dogs can be reverted back to sociable pets, so there is no need to give up on them too quickly.

Truly feral dogs may be a different story altogether. If a dog is truly feral, that is a puppy raised in the wild (without human contact) by a mother that was living in the wild, they will exhibit totally different characteristics from dogs that are temporarily living in the wild as a result of circumstances. We can see the difference in the dogs pretty clearly.

Feral dogs don't want to interact with humans and will not seek out human contact. When cornered, they often cower and look away and try their best to avoid capture. Feral dogs are difficult to domesticate even after the one-generation loss of domestication. Often these dogs are best cared for with TNR programs (trap neuter release) once spayed or neutered and vaccinated. This will of course depend on the area where the dog was found. Feral dogs can often survive on their own, scavenging food and gaining shelter. As is the situation with feral cats, it is a controversy within communities.

However, we must understand that dogs that are sometimes classified as feral are merely stray dogs that have lost some of their socialization skills. These are the dogs that we will address here. The puppies of feral dogs, if removed early enough, can be domesticated with little work. Most experts agree that 2-4 weeks of age is best to begin training and socializing feral puppies. The younger dogs will be less likely to run away from you, bite or learn feral traits from their mom if they are raised by humans and socialized properly. There are issues in removing domestic dogs from their mothers too early that create some behavioral challenges, but if we have no choice, this is the only option. Leaving feral puppies with feral mothers continues the feral characteristics that we are trying to change.

For the sake of this instruction, we will address "retraining" or "socializing" dogs that are first generation feral or dogs that are exhibiting feral tendencies, as opposed to those that are truly wild. These are the dogs that are shy of humans, reluctant to make contact, and are fearful and untrusting. With a bit of work, they can be managed and re-homed, and most of them can make good companions. I would suggest that they still be given generous time to develop and ample understanding of their core instincts, which can be triggered as a result of the feral experience.

The key to re-socializing these dogs is time and distance. The distance is the physical proximity to the dog and is similar to how we deal with desensitizing domestic dogs to people. With the feral nature, we focus more on allowing the dog to lose his premonitions instead of teaching him what we want him to learn.

- Upon first seeing the feral dog in a kennel, approach slowly and calmly. As with other desensitization techniques, no sounds should be made – especially no speaking or high-pitched sounds. Allow the dog to see you and just be in *his* vicinity. He will likely regress to the back of his kennel initially and look at you and then look away. Allow him to process the experience and remain neutral. Do not say anything and do not make direct eye contact.

- Once the dog seems indifferent to your presence, it is acceptable to enter the kennel and spend some time in there. Again, we want to keep our sounds and eye contact to an absolute minimum. We can begin with some soft whispering sounds or clicking sounds from our mouth. An occasional glimpse into the direction of the dog's face can be given, but again, no direct staring. We don't want to spook the dog or arouse his suspicions.

- If the dog is progressing well and accepting your presence without fear or dominance, place a bowl of food in one corner of the kennel and sit in the opposite corner. Don't sit next to the food or motion toward it. If the dog seems uncomfortable, remain neutral and avert his gaze. We are teaching him that there are two things in his proximity: something he is unfamiliar with (us) and something he likes (food). We don't need to be the *source* of that object (that is why we avoid hand-feeding at this point). He simply needs to learn that he is getting food and we are there – not doing anything –just being there.

- Within a few sessions, most dogs will begin coming closer to the human and reaching out. When they do, we sit calmly and allow them to sit close to us. We are looking for the dog to settle next to us and just lie down or relax. This is not the time to start playing with the dog, even if that is what we think he wants. The reason we want to avoid too much interaction here is because we don't want the dog to have a potentially bad experience. We want several neutral experiences to build up into a good experience. At this point, we can begin by throwing small bits of treats on the floor as he is sitting next to us. We do this slowly and indifferently. If he doesn't pay attention to the treats, we don't point to them or talk to him, "*Go get it.*" This is not what he is ready for. If he avoids the treats altogether, we leave them and stay neutral. He can get the treats after we leave. He will remember that the treats are a result of our visit and this should carry over to our next session.

- Once the dog has spent a couple of sessions sitting next to us in the kennel, we can begin gentle physical contact. Watch his body language, because if you've spent enough time, he will be open for it and probably sit close enough to touch you already. Once we can make physical contact, we can begin introducing a slip-lead and offer him treats while we show him the lead. If he is neutral enough, slip the lead over his head. If this works well, place the lead on and off of the dog's head several times before leading him out of the kennel. He should understand that the lead is nothing more than an object that will do him no harm.

- Once the dog has grown accustomed to the lead, we can bring him out of the kennel using the slip-lead and treats. Walk the dog indifferently toward a small fenced-in field and begin an interaction that involves keeping him focused on you.

If his focus remains on you, you can drop the lead and see if he returns to you. Every time he returns to you, reward him with praise or treats. If he tries to run, regain and maintain your hold on the lead and remain indifferent. Do not run after him. Simply wait until he is in an area where you can step on the lead that he is dragging and calmly pick it up. If he is fearful of something, don't try to talk him away from it. Instead, remain calm and wait for him to settle into the area and the surroundings. *Please read the section on desensitization to better understand this procedure.*

Once the *feral* dog is okay with human contact and interaction, we can work with his specific issues, instead of the issue being the feral dog himself. If he is afraid of bicycles, we can deal with that issue once we've moved past the issue of his feral nature. The dog that will now allow us to physically touch him and looks to us is on the road to recovery and we can desensitize him to outside stimuli if we have done the preliminary work to reverse his core feral traits.

Remember, the feral nature of the dog keeps him from interacting and trusting humans. Once he looks to the human, he is becoming a domesticated dog once again. Please read the sections on dealing with desensitization and training after completing the initial work of re-socializing the dog in the exercises above.

Removing Dogs from Kennels Safely

There are several risks in removing dogs from their kennels. Most of these risks can be eliminated, or at least drastically reduced.

The primary risk is the safety of our staff. Those not aware of the dog's overall personality face the greatest risk – injury to themselves if the dog is aggressive or high in drive. Employees are often bitten when trying to place a leash onto a dog that has issues. Therefore it's important to have kennel cards in place on the front door of each kennel, giving a glimpse into the dog's primary issues. These notes should be compiled from the staff behaviorist, dog walkers, volunteers and kennel workers.

To most easily classify dogs I recommend a *3-tier / 3-color system*.

Red Dogs – High Risk – These dogs should only be handled by top-level volunteers and shelter staff who have the training to do so.

Yellow Dogs – Medium Risk - These dogs have mild issues and may be handled by a mid-level staff or volunteers.

Green Dogs – Little or No Risk – These are dogs with no obvious issues and can be handled, walked and interacted with by anyone.

If we match volunteers with dogs, we can use the 3 color system on both. For example:

Red-level volunteers can handle all dogs: red, yellow and green.
Yellow-level volunteers can handle dogs labeled yellow and green.
Green-level volunteers can only handle green-level dogs.

I was confronted by a volunteer who was upset about this system at his shelter. He complained that he should be able to handle any of the dogs. I asked him why he would want to deal with the most difficult dogs when he could relax and have the best time with the nicest dogs. Once he understood the level of fun and benefit he could bring to the green dogs, he quickly recanted his complaint.

** These classifications can be easily displayed on the kennel card by a colored sticker or ribbon / tape on the door, as well as a tag on the dog's collar.

When approaching the kennel, I highly recommend a system of establishing structure before removing any dog. Taking this step, which only adds an extra 60-90 seconds to the procedure, can save lots of aggravation later on.

Step 1 – Approach the kennel, pause and squat outside the kennel. Wait for the dog to calm slightly.

Step 2 - When the dog calms, reward him with a treat.

Step 3 – Open the door and enter the kennel. **This should only be done with dogs that don't exhibit any aggression to humans, for obvious reasons. Once inside the kennel, remain calm and wait for the dog to show a bit more calmness. If the dog is jumping, remain still and wait for him to calm before slipping the lead around his neck. Although you may feel tempted to *just get it over with*, I encourage you to *wait*. Once the dog is a bit settled, place the lead around his neck, offer him a treat and open the kennel door.

Step 4 – In an ideal world we would like to have our dog walk on a perfect heel as we walk him out of the kennel and pass by other kennels with no reaction – but we all know this is highly unlikely. Instead, I keep a constant pace and don't let the dog interact too much with the other dogs. I will take a look at how reactive my dog is to the dogs in the other kennels. If he is overly reactive in an aggressive way, I will note that and use it in any further follow up assessment and notes. ** Just because a dog is reactive to another dog behind a barrier, does not necessarily indicate that this dog will be aggressive to that same dog once the barrier is removed.

** An alternative I often use and recommend to seasoned handlers still involves step 1 and 2, but changes at step 3. Instead of entering the kennel, I crack the door open and hold the slip-lead in an open position in front of the dog's head (sometimes it's beneficial to have a treat to lure the dog's head into and through the noose), as the dog moves his head forward, I drop the noose and maintain my hold on the line and the lead tightens on the dog's neck as he moves through. I use this procedure on dogs that I don't feel will be an issue.

The last thing you want is to lose a dog when removing it from the kennel. There are several problems that can arise, including the dog injuring himself, coming into contact with another problematic dog, getting out of the shelter altogether, or scaring potential adopters. It's best to always be cautious when removing a dog from a kennel and taking the time to build some sort of engagement with the dog will give you a bit of an edge later on.

Minimizing Injuries

As I've mentioned several times in this book, the issue of primary importance should be the safety of our staff, trainers and volunteers. Without a well-structured procedure for dealing with dogs, we cannot save any. We want to assure that people dealing with dogs are qualified – as well as physically and emotionally capable of handling these responsibilities.

If a well-intentioned staff member gets bitten by a dog, he will be unable to help other dogs. Also, the dog he was working with will usually end up on a bite quarantine, so it is better to be safe than sorry when dealing with *all* dogs. Since all dogs share the likelihood to bite, all dogs should be approached the in the same way– until we know for certain. "*Thinking*" that a certain dog is *OK* is a big problem. Don't think – make certain, and when you are certain, continue to be careful. This has always been my motto in training, evaluating and in teaching. We're never 100% certain of any dog, so always exercise caution.

Anyone handling dogs should be physically fit enough to handle the dogs they are dealing with. It makes no sense to allow someone to handle a large dog with behavioral issues if they cannot physically control *that* dog. This doesn't disqualify women from handling large dogs, because I've seen plenty of female trainers better suited to handle large dogs than many men. Besides the physical ability, there are techniques that can give a strong edge to the right handler, the key one being a clear mental edge and ability to read a dog.

Mistakes can be costly - As I stated above, a mistake can cost us a physical injury and possibly the dog his life. I opt to err on the side of caution when approaching any new dog. Anyone handling a dog should be instructed to go slowly and carefully on any and all dogs that have not been tested. Dogs' personalities can shift, depending on environmental conditions. The stress of being in a shelter can turn even a calm dog into a dog that might snap.

No hugs Possibly my number 1 complaint is seeing people physically handling dogs in coddling ways. Dogs that don't know you will, at best, tolerate physical contact. Hugging and kissing dogs puts them into a stressful situation and can cause a dog to try and break free. This can result in bites and/or scratches to the person handling them. This holds true for small and large dogs, and the concept of "It never happened before" is no excuse. It is our goal to avoid the potential for injury, not to hope that no injury occurs. So anyone hugging and *holding* dogs should be corrected and lectured on safety. There is no excuse for hugging dogs we don't know – except for our selfish emotions.

Your head, not your hands – If a dog fight occurs, do NOT place your hands near either dog's mouth to stop the fight, even if a larger dog has a smaller dog in his mouth. Dogs are known to bite whatever is in front of them, and placing your hand there is a sure fire way to get bit. You can use any other item and put that in front of the dog to redirect his bite, but NOT your hand.

Leashing - When leashing a dog, it is always best to use a slip-line. This keeps you from needing to make excessive contact with the dog. Placing the line over his head is simple because the noose can be opened as big as required and can be cinched quickly. I suggest tossing a few treats to the dog to "neutralize" his initial experience with a new person in his kennel.

If you can't, don't - Staff should never be *made to deal* with dogs that they can't handle. If you have a question about a particular dog and you don't feel safe, the answer is DON'T. Don't take unnecessary chances. If you can't get someone else to handle the dog you are unsure of, at the very least have someone with you. If a dog must be removed from a kennel and is unmanageable, the options are either to use a pole or to sedate the dog before handling him.

Protective clothing – Shorts, open-toe shoes and clothes that don't cover enough skin should not be permitted for those handling animals. Gloves are a good idea to prevent burns from ropes and minimizing injury to hands. Baggy clothes should be avoided as well, as they present an opportunity for a dog to latch onto something – be it in play or drive.

216

B.A.R.C.
Behavioral Assessment & Reactivity Checklist

Developed by: Robert Cabral -
Bound Angels / Black Belt Dog Training

The premise of the canine temperament test has been widely disputed among animal rights people due to the unfair elements imposed on the dog. The primary reason for this controversy is the blanket "pass or fail" method that is applied to the outcome of the test. Assessing a dog's behavior should not be gauged *pass or fail*; rather we should strive to define the dog's behavior. We must use the test as a litmus to understand the dog's true temperament. To more clearly understand this, let's define the term "temperament."

To equate the word to a human level, we can define temperament as a dog's "personality." Seeing it in these terms, we should be able to clearly define what a dog's strong and weak traits are, and how to properly address them. For example, a dog that is fearful of other dogs or even dominant toward them is not a dog that should be put down, but it would be good to know this information before placing him into a home with other dogs, or with a weak handler. Rather, this dog should be placed with a rescue organization that could work at rehabilitating the dog. If we can assess a dog's needs, we can offer better solutions to place him in an environment best suited for him.

217

Although this test is designed to be as detailed as possible, we must understand that a dog is a living, breathing, ever-changing animal that may react one way during a test and differently once placed in a different environment. A great example of this is the likelihood of a dog acting more dominant around a weaker handler and less dominant around someone who is firmer. Dogs are conditioned by their environment, as well as by the people and animals that surround them.

If a test were performed in a completely sterile environment, the results would be useless because we never place our dogs in a truly sterile environment. The test is designed to give us a snapshot of a dog's personality, and as responsible people we must use this information in the best interest of the dog being tested.

It is my contention that few, if any dogs, should ever be killed because of aggression issues. More than 90% of dominance and aggression can be treated through proper behavior modification by a qualified trainer or behaviorist. Much of this can be done with positive, reward-based methods, but we should not rule out correction-based training if it is the sole option to saving a dog's life. I would rather put a correction upon a dog than a needle in his vein. To say otherwise is playing God for an animal that deserves every option before a last resort.

My contention is that all training should start with a treat and a toy; where it goes from there is up to the individual dog. Training a dog, that is, teaching dog basic commands (i.e., sit, stay, down, come, etc.) should only be done through motivational methods. Enforcement of commands once we know the dog understands what we want can employ well-suited corrections, as long as they are fair to the dog. My opinion is that a correction is merely a *direction* for a dog to do what I'm trying to get him to do. For example, if a dog that I'm handling is pulling toward another dog and I say, NO, I can give a leash correction to take the dog away from that situation, thereby "correcting" him into compliance.

Thousands of dogs are killed every year for a plethora of reasons, some of which include bad behavior. If even a small percentage of them could be saved by proper behavioral evaluations, our work will be worthwhile. Furthermore, if we can offer another small percentage of these dogs another chance at life by instilling good behavior into them, it would be the greatest gift. All too often, people approach dogs with a blanket opinion, such as, "If the dog will not change his behavior through positive based methods, he will not change." Others say that correction-based training doesn't retain its strength. I would argue that, with much experience to the contrary. I have trained many dogs with correction-based methods (because the motivational techniques would not work due to the immense drive of the particular dog) and these dogs have maintained their good behavior over many years. These dogs showed serious aggression issues prior to training and are now living happy lives.

We must step outside of our egos and give the dog what he needs, not what we think he needs.

A word of caution to those performing the behavioral assessment test: Working with a dog that exhibits dominant or aggressive behaviors cannot be compared to performing a test on an unknown dog. Dogs can behave erratically or out of control during a behavioral assessment. There is an inherent risk of being bitten during a test, so extreme caution should be used. Do not let your guard down during any part of the test.

A note on underlying issues: There are several things that can sway a dog negatively in a behavioral assessment test, and it's imperative that they be addressed here:

A dog should not be tested immediately upon entering the shelter. The dog is in a highly stressed state and may react out of confusion. A test conducted on a dog within 12-24 hours of entering the shelter is not deemed valid. Dogs that are sick, including kennel cough or after any surgery requiring anesthesia, should not be tested until they are well or at least 48 hours after surgery. If recovery is necessary (for example, setting a broken bone or major surgery) the dog must be fully recovered, with no touch sensitivity before testing. If the dog is tested with stitches or staples still intact, the area in question must be avoided.

Dogs should not be tested immediately after feeding time and should not be removed from feeding for testing. Furthermore, a dog should not be tested in the proximity of other dogs that are eating.

Dogs should not be tested in the immediate vicinity of kennel mates still in the kennel. If dogs have issues with hip dysplasia, this issue should be taken into account and disclosed on the test.

The Tester: Having performed hundreds of these tests, I can confirm that no dog will respond the exact same way to two different people. In order to be fair to the dog, we must be sure that the dog has no blanket issue with the person performing the behavioral test. When I say blanket issue, I mean overly negative or positive. The best person to conduct a test is a person who can detach himself or herself from the task at hand and handle a dog neutrally.

If a dog really seems to like someone, that person may be likely to get inaccurate results on some parts of the test; however, a negative pre-association to the tester is the most important aspect we should focus to avoid.

The tester's background need not to be a medical one. Some trainers make great testers - some don't. Some people may be too wishy-washy to deal with a strong dog at a moment's notice, while others are so dominant in tone that they cannot get a dog to relax enough in order to be playful or to exhibit his true personality. The tester must be neutral to "his favorite breed." Playing favorites or skewing a test because the handler is not a fan of the breed is unfair and has no place in a behavioral test. The level of energy spent dealing with the first dog should be the same as with the last; therefore it is advisable to consider how many tests the person can perform before requiring a break or ending testing for a given day. I've tested 15-20 dogs in a 3-4 hour time frame, for a basic test, while other dogs have consumed many hours over several days in order to get a fair idea of the dog's personality.

The tester is equally capable as a man or a woman and most any age. I look for a couple of qualifications for the person doing the test. The most important is the person's ability to read a dog. This generally comes with much experience in dealing with dogs that may have personality disorders. Dog trainers who spend most of their time in clients' homes often don't have the ability to read a dog that may exhibit behavioral issues – be they good or bad.

The attire of the person testing should allow them to interact freely with the dog. I generally wear jeans, boots and a t-shirt. If a person has sensitive skin, I suggest wearing a long-sleeved shirt or thin jacket to avoid getting scratched. Bulky clothes will inhibit movement, and freedom of movement is imperative when interacting with the dog. The reason I suggest a firm shoe or boot is that some dogs may become nippy at feet, and sneakers or sandals will leave our feet open to the dogs' "attacks" - regardless of if they are playful or serious. I also suggest avoiding clothing that makes rustling noises (such as nylon jackets) as this may distract a dog during the test.

The tester should be strong enough to control a dog at a moment's notice and compassionate enough to give each dog tested a fair chance.

The Testing Environment: Testing a dog at a shelter is not a perfect scenario. There are so many smells and sounds that trigger a dog to react in a way that may sway the test. This sway can be for the good or bad. Some dogs may respond aggressively in this environment and passively in a more neutral environment. Therefore, when testing at a shelter, I advocate for a field or area away from the medical, exam and intake area – as well as away from the main kennel area of the shelter whenever possible. If this is not possible, try to be as far away as you can..

How the dog is brought to the testing area will also influence the outcome. I suggest that a dog be brought from its kennel to the test area in a neutral manner. There should be no talking, petting or jerking the dog around. If the dog decides to engage in cage fighting, move the dog straight along. Correcting the dog incites a behavior in his mind that will sway the test, as well as his experience with the handler.

My initial method to meeting the dog to be tested

is to approach the kennel, give the dog a treat or just drop a treat on the floor of the kennel and stand there for a brief moment. I always use a noose to secure the dog, generally luring him to the front of the kennel and then taking him out. If he is skittish, I will enter the kennel and noose him from there – again, my attitude remains very aloof. No matter how fearful or dominant the dog acts, I do not engage in any dialog or training methods at this point. If the dog is posturing, I do not approach him straight on; instead I approach from the side.

I do not like to use a catchpole on a dog, and up to now have never felt the need to use one in a test. The experience of the pole places a negative imprint on the dog that will impact the results of our test. If the dog cannot be safely handled by use of a simple noose, we need to give the dog more time or bring him into an area where he can be handled with a noose.

Once the dog is on the rope, we walk past the other dogs and get to the training or testing area as quickly as possible, and with as little drama as possible.

Once in the testing area, I leave the leash on the dog and allow him to run free for a few moments. If you are using a simple noose leash, I suggest you tie a knot above the ring to avoid the dog slipping out or getting his feet tangled. Some of the shepherd's leashes have a small piece of leather that can be slipped down to avoid loosening of the collar. In either case, I prefer to leave the dog on the leash during the entire test; I suggest you do the same.

More than likely, the dog will enjoy this initial bit of freedom and we can see if he runs up to other people in the testing area (although they should remain neutral and not engage the dog). He may also become fixated on something or he may need to relieve himself.

Possession test: At this point I want to see how possessive the dog is over a particular toy or object. Is his possessiveness over a particular toy or is he possessive over anything that he believes is his? The key to testing possessiveness with a dog is to always offer him another toy or reward of equal or greater value when trying to remove the first object. Just trying to yank a toy from a dog's mouth does not prove possessiveness, at least not on the dog's side. Offering him other items shows his dedication to the object he is currently dealing with. Also, if this item has him fixated, I may re-introduce it later to see if he will *lock* onto it again.

Most dogs are able to strike an object with a bite if it is moving in a normal *charged* manner. A big mistake people make is moving an item in an erratic manner when introducing it to the dog. The dog may inadvertently bite the skin or hand of the handler and thereby fail his test. This is not a failure for the dog, but more a failure of the handler. Introducing an item on a string that we can toss or *activate* on the ground serves as the best introduction of a toy. Furthermore, if I activate the toy, that is pull on it while the dog has a hold on it, the dog's natural instinct will be to pull back. You will not get an object out of a dog's mouth by pulling on it against the dog's grip, nor will you free the object by having someone yanking back on the dog while you are holding the object. The way to free the object through compulsion is to use a collar correction from the front of the dog while pulling or holding onto the object. However, I do not do this during a temperament test, as this leads into training and behavior modification. The idea of a test is to remain neutral.

Dogs that go from toy to toy are perfectly suited in normal behavior and show a high level of curiosity. Dogs that fixate on an object and cannot be pulled away from that object – no matter what the secondary reward is – are quite rare but show a strong dedication and drive. Dogs that bite or attack when approached while playing need to be schooled in the proper etiquette of play. This is not a reason to kill a dog; it's merely a personality trait that generally can be fixed.

There are different approaches to separating a dog from the object he is possessing:

- Remove the object from the dog while securing (or having another person secure) the dog. Offer a second item to the dog to make a swap.

- The best method is not to remove the

item from the dog, but instead remove the dog from the item. If I use this method, I can bring the dog back to the item and see if his level of drive or possessiveness has gone up, down or remained the same.

If a dog growls when approached while playing with an item, he is exhibiting resource-guarding tendencies. These tendencies are prevalent in strong personality dogs and can often be quite useful in bite sports. If a dog snaps when approached, a correction should be delivered and the situation should be repeated.

Dogs that resource-guard to an extreme extent can be retrained through both motivational- and correction-based training. Although it is a rare trait in all but a few dogs, resource-guarding is a behavioral issue that needs to be addressed. What is important here is to clearly differentiate between a dog that is truly guarding to attack, from one that is growling in a manner to initiate continuation of play. This can generally be observed by noting the body language of the dog: Still body, hackles up, stiffness and eyes peering up are signs the dog is guarding and remaining possessive over the item. Loose energy, flexible body and mid-level growling while moving away from the item or holding it is a general indication that he wishes the game to continue.

Next, I will introduce a few toys, tugs or treats to see how the dog responds. I watch how the dog responds to me, the environment and to each item that I bring out of my bag as I retain an indifferent attitude. I do not start a play session with the dog at this point. I am merely looking at the dog's curiosity or drive toward the items I am handling. Is he excited, curious, pushy or indifferent?

I will throw a toy and see if he chases it, then I will throw another toy. Does he immediately go for the other toy and forget about the first? If not, I will approach him and offer him a treat or another toy from my hand to see if he'll give up the current toy. If not, I will grab hold of the toy and hold it. I do not pull it, jerk it or tug on it. I merely deaden the object. The best toy to use for this is a tug or ball on a string.

To avoid getting bitten, I secure a hold of the leash or noose the dog has been wearing the entire time. When you deaden an object, a dog will generally lose interest and let go. If he lets go, I throw it for him again and let him chase it. This shows that a dog has a natural prey drive and he is acting very normal. A dog that holds onto a toy that I have secured in my hand is not necessarily an aggressive dog; instead he is showing an engagement to me.

If a dog snaps when you grab the toy he is holding, this could be seen as aggression or "re-biting" – something a dog does to get a firmer hold on the object. If the dog "re-bites" the object, keep the object motionless and see he loses interest. A dog may "re-bite" an object a number of times before losing interest. If the dog snarls, growls or postures when you handle the object, we see this as a dominant tendency and he should be given a fair correction to see if he responds. Failing a dog due to possessiveness without offering him a fair correction is throwing the baby out with the bathwater. It is our job to read a dog for his personality, and some dogs require a slight correction to fall into line. If the dog becomes aggressive or continues his dominance, he is showing some tendencies toward possessiveness.

Depending on the level of the dog's possessiveness, I will present another object to the dog to see if he feigns interest in it. When testing a dog for possessiveness, we should see what the dog is possessive toward (food, toys, etc.). A dog with possession issues will continue to be possessive over an object even if we think he's lost interest in it. In his mind, he sees everything as his and no one can touch any of his possessions. That is why using multiple objects as a replacement gives us insight as to the dog's true drive.

Although there are ways to separate the item from the dog in a compulsive manner, we should not be concerned with this during a temperament test. If we can't get the item away from the dog during the test with the above explanation(s), then one of two things is true:

1. We are not qualified to handle this particular dog.

2. The dog is truly a difficult dog and should be rescue only and placed in a behavior modification program.

I would venture to say that more than likely #1 holds true for most situations. Unless a dog assaults with a bite or attack for trying to get the object away from him, there are many ways to get the object away from him. Please see previous sections of this book for more detailed explanations.

The touch / handling test: To start, we should understand that dogs don't generally like to be handled –that is often the reason why children get bit by dogs when they crawl on top of them and parents do nothing to stop it. I do not blame dogs for responding in this way, since it is a part of their natural behavior. Hugging dogs, lying on top of them, pinning them, or excessive handling makes dogs feel the need to break free. Bearing this in mind, there are several things that I will look for in the handling test.

Step 1. I start with the dog on the noose and offer him a treat. I will touch him gently on the head and move my way down the body. I touch the back, sides and underside of the dog. I will apply slight pressure to the front shoulders and back hips. I will stroke his tail and I may hold it for a brief moment. All of this is done while I maintain control of the rope attached to the dog's neck. It is important that there be enough slack in the rope to keep the dog from feeling tension, but the slack should be short enough to allow the handler to gain immediate control of the dog if he turns to bite. If he does turn to bite, our reaction should be indifferent. We can correct the dog and protect ourselves, but getting emotional or angry is not part of our job on this test. If we see that the issue is fear-based, we can spend some time reassuring the dog and repeating the touch test to the sensitive area(s).

Most items covered here will elicit a unique response in different dogs. A dog that does not like to be touched can still be a good pet, but probably should not be placed with small children. Dogs that have hindquarter sensitivity or tail-handling issues also are not a good fit for children.

Again, the goal of a proper behavioral assessment is to clearly define the best home for a dog. By giving a dog a grade, we offer him a chance and open up space for other dogs.

Step 2. When testing the *touch phase*, I will also approach the dog from the rear, as some dogs spook easily when people do this. Some dogs will just turn around with surprise and then recover. The key to this is that the tester must remain neutral. If the tester spooks at the *dog's reaction*, the dog may nip or move forward, and rightfully so. Approaching a dog and then regressing elicits a forward motion from the dog (prey drive). If you approach the average dog and then regress, you will find that the dog moves forward. Similarly moving forward (as in chasing the dog) generally elicits a recoiling movement from the dog.

Step 3. During the touch phase, if I see a neutral or playful reaction from the dog I will continue on with the test. Next, I try to lift the dog's front paws and hold them for a brief moment. Slight pressure will show if there is any sensitivity in the dog's paws, which might require medical attention. I will also reward each touch with a reward, namely a treat. I want to remain fair to the dog and when a dog sees he's getting rewarded, he will more than likely go along with the test and not become irritated. There is no logic to testing a dog's limit unless you want the dog to fail. People who continue with a barrage of assaults on the dog, including pokes, jabs and overt handling are forcing a dog to fail. The test must remain neutral, and keeping the dog calm is the simplest way to keep the test neutral for the dog. If a dog responds positively when I act positively, I know his personality. Similarly, if a dog reacts negatively to me when I approach positively, I can be clear that there may be a problem.

Step 4. I will move along and see if the dog allows all of his paws and legs to be handled. If so, I continue. Remember, that a dog who offers his front legs is showing submission, rear legs have no indication of submission and are often more likely to elicit a different response. However, a dog that allows you to pick up all of his paws is generally a very solid dog, with few issues. This is rare, but there are dogs like this.

Step 5. With smaller dogs, I will try lifting them off of the ground to see how they respond to handling. Although I feel that carrying a dog is wrong unless it is injured, I do include it in my test because so many people insist on carrying smaller dogs. A dog should remain relaxed when I pick him up. Dogs that become stiff are not comfortable being picked up and should not be pushed any further.

Step 6. Although I am vehemently against pulling a dog's tail, I include it in my test because of the irresponsible parents who may not tell their child that this is wrong. Some dogs have a big issue with it. I watch the dog's head carefully as I grab hold of the tail and tug slightly. If the dog turns to bite, a good hold on his tail can protect you from getting bitten. However, you should still have hold of the leash with your other hand.

Step 7. Ears and eyes. To test a dog's ears and eyes, I squat next to the dog and rub his head and move over to the ears, lifting them up and gently massage them. I bring my hand forward toward the dog's nose and cover one eye at a time to see the dog's reaction. Ideally, the dog will not respond. A common response is for the dog to squirm his head around to move out from under your hand. If the dog does this more than once, he is not comfortable with eye handling and that should be noted. It is not a negative in any manner, unless the dog becomes aggressive or reactive.

Step 8. Mouth. I will rub the dog's head and move my hand toward his mouth. If he's fine, I can use my fingers to open the dog's lips and immediately offer him a treat. I'll repeat this on both sides. A dog that allows you to handle his mouth is another very rare candidate and getting this info will give us a stronger indication of a dog's limits. It's important to be extremely careful when handling a dog's mouth with your hands. I suggest watching for any indications, and if they arise, abort this portion of the test. There is no sense in getting bitten to prove a point.

As you may note, I offer a treat to a dog for compliance. This is important for the dog to see that he is being tested and not bribed. If he is truly a problem dog, he will respond negatively, whether I offer him a treat or not. Offering him a reward gives us a fair idea of his compliance. Those who argue that giving treats during a test sways the results are biased toward failing dogs in these tests.

Food test: Perhaps the worst aspect of temperament testing that has ever been introduced is the use of a plastic hand to test a dog for food aggression. I could write a book on this topic alone, but I'll withhold my litany and just say that it is idiotic for many reasons. The primary reason is that a dog that is eating should not be disturbed. For those people who think that this "test" is important because children may approach a dog while he is eating, I suggest that you train children not to interfere with a dog that is eating. Furthermore, a dog that bites a plastic hand is biting an object that has absolutely no relation to a human hand; he may or may not bite a hand, but the plastic one gives us no clear indication. You can use a broomstick or pipe with the exact same results.

Since dogs are creatures of scent, we are betraying the dog's strongest drive by introducing a plastic prosthetic because – whether it looks like a hand or not – it's not a human hand to the dog. Remember, there is no need to reach into a dog's bowl while he is eating – NONE! Dogs that have food issues may have a right to have these issues: if a dog has been at the shelter and has not had enough to eat or has lived in the streets where food is in short supply, he may exhibit behaviors that he has learned to keep him alive. I am more interested in a dog's food issues as they relate to other dogs, as opposed to humans. Furthermore, retraining a dog to lose biting tendencies toward people (not children) is not impossible. Therefore, with a little work we can fix a problem that would otherwise be a death sentence for a dog.

I test a dog for food issues using my hands and treats in a much different and much fairer way. I offer the dog a treat and let him take it from my hand. Then I offer another and partially remove it. I want to see the dog's drive in trying to get the treat back. Will he back down or pursue my hand for the treat? I want to see how the dog takes the treat from my hand. This will show me that the dog can differentiate my hand from a treat, and it also reveals his level of drive for food. I watch a dog's behavior when I have food in my hand, as well as when I reach into my bag or pouch for more food. I may even eat in front of the dog and watch his drive.

Follow these steps in order, and do not progress to the next step if the dog is reacting adversely in the current step.

Step 1. When the dog approaches, offer him a treat, preferably something about 3-6 inches long, such as a strip of jerky. Allow the dog to bite it off or break it off when it is in his mouth.

Step 2. Offer the dog another treat and, as he begins to bite down, pull the treat back out of his mouth. What is his reaction? Confusion? Regression? Assertiveness?

Step 3. Drop a piece of the treat on the ground and as soon as the dog sees it, cover it with your foot. Observe the reaction: Confusion? (Looking up to you.) Assertiveness? (Digging at the treat.) Indifference? (*Hopefully you are wearing boots.*)

Step 4. When the dog is eating the treat, begin some mild general handling (head patting, body contact, moving around). If he's steady and comfortable with you, he will continue eating the treat from your hand. If he gets confused, he will stop and back up. If he becomes irritated, he may growl or snap your hand.

Step 5. Initiate some mouth handling while the dog is eating the treat. I begin touching lips, chin, and nose and cover his eyes. These are trigger areas, but we are approaching them in a manner that is fair to the dog. The best result to see is a dog that remains focused on the food and pays little attention to your handling. Remember, you will not proceed to this step if the dog showed any adverse reaction in the previous step(s).

Step 6. Introduce another dog into the immediate (but not reachable) vicinity of the dog. Begin offering the other dog treats while the *test dog* is ignored. He should be close enough to see the other dog being fed, but not close enough to connect. At this point, if the dog has shown favorable responses to the rest of this test I move forward and bring the two dogs closer together. I will drop some treats for one dog, and immediately reach across and drop some for the other dog. I generally will do this with an assistant or I will tie one dog off to a pole. It will be nearly impossible to handle both dogs during this test and dispense food and watch for behaviors. Be diligent in this test – it will be an important part of the evaluation.

If your dog moves toward the other dog in a dominant manner, he should be corrected and reintroduced immediately. By *dominant* it is understood that the dog is going after the other dog and not the food, and he is going after the other dog in order to get the food. The dogs should be able to take treats at the same time from the ground or should ignore the treats while the other dog eats. Both of these are highly favorable responses.

The correction here should be in the form of a leash correction, showing the dog that this behavior is not acceptable. To simply disqualify the dog for showing some food dominance is highly unfair. Once corrected, I've found that most dogs will settle down and share the treats or ignore the other dog. A dog that shows possessiveness toward food can be retrained, or an easier solution to the problem is to insist on a separate feeding area for the dog. Dogs in shelters are often very food possessive. This is in no way a red-strike against the dog; it is merely an observation toward better understanding of how to handle this particular dog.

Correction test: How a dog responds to basic corrections on a leash is a good indication of how well he will be able to adjust to many social environments. Using the noose that we've left on the dog during the entire test, I will walk the dog around the field, near other people and near distractions. I will let the dog sniff something for a few moments and then give a slight tug on the leash followed, by a verbal direction. Here I look for his immediate and secondary responses.

Upon administering the correction, I look to see if he redirects his attention to me, which is what I'm looking for. Does he drop in fear, does his tail go between his legs or does his back become hunched? Does he completely ignore me and keep doing what he's doing? Or does he redirect toward me? That is to say, does he turn to bite the person who delivered the correction? Any reaction but the last one is okay. A dog that redirects and tries to bite the person delivering a slight redirection should be looked at further.

It is important that the correction be a tug on the leash, not a crushing blow. It will need to be scaled from smaller dogs to larger dogs and should be at the level to merely get the dog's attention away from what he is focused on. The rarest of dogs
(I'd say less than 1 in 500) will redirect and try to bite the handler.

Dominance test: I want to be clear here that I suggest testing a dog for dominance without drawing a conclusion that a dominant dog is a bad dog. All dogs have a level of dominance and testing for *it* is paramount to understanding the dog. As a tester, I consider it my obligation to know what the dog will and will not tolerate. For example, if I am testing a dog that will be handled by children, I will grab the dog's tail and give it a slight tug. Yes, this may be a silly test, but I know for a fact that a child will pull a dog's tail given the chance, and if the parents are too ignorant to teach a child not to, I want to know what the dog's reaction will be. If the dog gets crazy from a tail pulling, I would note that and would not place the dog with small children.

Again, these tests are not to disqualify a dog from "passing or failing," simply to disqualify the dog from a home that would be unsuitable for the dog. Often times I will test a dog to see *when* he bites instead of *if* he bites. When I can find the threshold of the dog, I feel I know the dog. This isn't something I suggest for everyone, but for people with intensive experience it is a good tool.

If you're clear that the dog is dominant, it is a bad idea to do the following tests, as you may get bitten. These tests are to classify a dog as dominant if we are uncertain, and if he displays dominant tendencies during the test, what will be his reaction? Will he move away to avoid or will he strike back?

Step 1. Push down on a dog's shoulders using your hand and forearm. Submissive dogs will melt down under slight pressure or slide away. A dominant dog will rear up or remain still and motionless in a way to communicate that he is about to attack.

Step 2. Directly stare at the dog's eyes. This is a test that sets off a dog's trigger, but because people do it, we test for it. Many dogs will look away or will engage with play barking. The dogs that get very still and begin snarling are the trigger we're looking to classify.

Step 3. Reach underneath a dog's backside. To do this, I start on the back leg and move up toward the inside of the thigh. We covered this in the previous handling section, but I want to re-address it here because a dominant dog will not tolerate it. If a dog becomes fidgety when you move up the inside of his/her leg it is not a dominant dog. Dominant dogs become still or will immediately snap. Be certain that the dog you are testing is secured and you are able to quickly move away. It is probably best to do this with a savvy dog handler helping you.

Step 4. Remove a toy from a dog's proximity or mouth. Again, another topic that I covered previously, but I want to see the dog's reaction. If you are removing the item from the dog, I suggest you have the dog restrained in a manner that will limit his mobility as you reach in. A better way, depending if one is available, is to use a helper who will be able to pull the dog back and away from you if the dog strikes. Be certain that the person has keen reflexes and the strength to keep the dog from getting to you.

Closed environment test: This section can be done at the beginning or end of the test. I generally use the kennel for this or a corner of the field. I want to see how the dog responds to small areas or confinement. I don't advise this test with dogs that have already displayed territorial issues.

The first thing I look for is how the dog will respond to my approaching him when he is in a corner. Many dogs will dart out and go to another area of the kennel. Others will become very submissive. Still others will posture and make it known that they will attack.

To handle this in a fair manner, it is important to be neutral on the approach and not directly confront the dog – in particular a dog that is already showing signs of adverse behavior to the environment. If you *storm* the area and the dog reacts and then label the dog as territorially aggressive, it's a highly unfair assessment. We want to see if the dog is truly exhibiting issues about the environment first, and not about our approach to it.

In order to achieve this, we offer the dog a small treat, usually thrown to them. We do not engage in verbal interaction with the dog. If the dog takes the treat and his body language becomes more open, we continue. After a few moments, we approach closer and closer to see at which point the dog becomes responsive to our encroachment. If the dog never becomes open and continues to posture in a fearful or dominant manner, we will try to move the dog to another area of confinement to see if the behavior is specific to his current environment or the overall concept of confinement.

If he is only reactive to his personal environment, we will need to spend some time working him on territorial issues. If it is every area, it is generally an issue of fear, which can be addressed through basic structure training. Dogs that outright attack when you approach their areas are the ones of great concern. This response is generally seen in dogs that were previously *chained.* Retraining *this* is possible, but a bit of work, depending on their level of aggression.

Loud noise / startle response: Loud noises can illicit several reactions in dogs: neutrality, assertion, curiosity or withdrawal. If a dog is easily spooked by loud noises, he may be fearful and may react adversely in stimulating environments. This can include a car backfiring, thunder, slamming doors, dropping an item on the floor, loud music, etc. Also, dogs that become fearful or reactive to loud noises may become spooked. We do not worry if a dog responds through withdrawal: instead we are looking for a heavily skewed reaction such as growling or immediate posturing. A dog may get spooked by a loud noise and pull away, then immediately return in a curious manner. This is a very positive sign.

Many dogs that are used for police work, bite sports; SAR, etc., are generally acclimated to loud noises at an early age. It is important that these types of dogs are neutral to loud sounds because they will encounter them on a regular basis. One of the most desired responses is a reaction to the initial sound and then a curious, investigative follow up.

To test a dog for this, I do the following:

- When the dog is focused on a toy or a treat, I drop a metal bowl about 2-3 feet away from its head on a cement floor. If there is only grass, I use two bowls and clang them together.

- Slam a kennel door as the dog walks out or walks by.

- As the dog is walking through the kennel, I'll knock something over as he walks by. This can be a broom, a wet floor sign or anything.

- When the dog is focused on someone or something in the testing area a loud clap about 2-3 feet behind his head.

It is important that the dog not recognize that the sounds are related to you. When the dog turns toward you, the object (for example, the bowl you dropped) should be out of your hands. If you clanged two bowls together, move them behind your back immediately after making the noise.

This test can be repeated a few times with different items and different locations. It is important to note that the *noise test* is looking for what is called a *startle response.* All too often, people test dogs for startle response by throwing something at the dog. This is incorrect because it is a direct threat to the dog. The dog should not feel any threat by the item. That is why it is best to have the sound "just happen."

If we see a sharp (or negative) response from the dog, we can move along in the test and add another startle test a little later on. On the subsequent noises, the dog should become more accustomed to the sounds and react with less and less surprise.

It is important to remember that there is no failing on this section of the test because the dog becomes fearful or jolted by the response. The only negative response is a dog that will turn toward aggression when startled by a sound.

Some people test a dog's startle response by poking him when he's not looking. I find this to be an unnecessary test unless the dog is going to a home with uncontrollable small children, which I don't believe is a suitable home for any dog. It is as unfair as running up behind you and smacking you and seeing what your response is. Behavioral assessment tests must, above all, be fair.

Other dogs: Introducing dogs to other dogs is a science in and of itself. Just because a dog reacts negatively to another dog through a cage or fence is no indication that the dog will show this same reaction when the barrier is removed. Also, some dogs display aggression toward other dogs when they themselves are on a leash but will not act aggressively when in a free environment. These indications are generally due to improper socialization and are important things to note during our test. It is not a good idea to simply take two dogs and put them together in a yard to put this concept to the test. We strive to introduce two dogs in a fair manner and see their personality.

We should start by understanding that certain dogs will respond in certain ways. Dominant dogs will posture and assume a position. Male to female interaction can elicit a sexual posture. My position is generally to introduce like- sex dogs for basic temperament testing. The reason for this is, that like-sex fights tend to be the most common and most problematic.

A crucial aspect of the dog-to-dog test is that the dog we are testing our candidate against should be neutral. If the other dog is high-strung, overly fearful, dominant or very reactive, the test is highly unfair. A good testing dog is hard to find, and once found is worth his weight in gold.

I start the test through the fence and always make sure that the person handling the other dog in the yard is competent and able to understand my directions. I also want a person who will follow my direction at a moment's notice and not stall, which could cause serious injury to both dog and tester.

I will walk through the gate and into the yard,

and then go my way while my assistant holds her dog on a stay. I watch my dog for any indication of curiosity. I walk my dog by the other dog a couple of times, and if the other dog is a good helper (not lunging, growling, barking or acting up), I will allow my dog to go over and greet him. I do not let them meet if either or both of them are too excited. I keep my leash loose and ask my assistant to do the same with hers. Again, I only allow this if I see that the dogs are neutral. If they are not, I will walk away and reintroduce. I do not introduce two dogs that are high-strung. The sniffing or introduction lasts only a few moments (a count of 3-5 is often enough). Then I remove my dog or have my assistant remove hers.

When I say *remove* the dog, I do NOT yank them away from each other, as this can create a negative response or experience. This response will be a direct response to the way the dog was removed, *not* a response to the other dog. If all goes well, I will go back over and reintroduce, then move the dogs apart and stroke the other dog's head. I'm looking for a reaction in my dog. I'm looking for neutrality. I will take this as far as feeding them both treats when they are sitting close to each other. I do, however, always assure that I have enough time and space to pull the dogs apart in the event that they become territorial or aggressive. If it is necessary to separate two dogs that are becoming aggressive, it should be done in a firm yet unemotional manner. There should be no yelling or explaining. The dogs are separated and reintroduced.

I've performed tests in which I had to reintroduce two dogs 4 to 5 times before they understood that they should get along. In these situations I can put a note on the dog's file that the dog *can* be fine with other dogs if he is introduced properly. There are certain dogs that – even with proper introduction – cannot get along with another dog. Again, this should be noted. Most dogs have no issues with other dogs, if properly introduced. The shelter environment is not the best place to properly introduce two dogs if they have issues.

The most important thing to watch for in dog-to-dog testing is that the leashes don't get tangled. If they do, you have a major issue. Pulling on tangled leashes is a certain way to get two dogs to engage. Reaching in to separate them while the dogs are engaged is a certain way to get bit. If, during a test the leashes get tangled, I will drop my leash, grab a toy or treat and call my dog to me at the same time I ask my assistant to stand still. The faster I can back away, the faster the dog will try to follow. I would suggest that you be extremely careful to avoid leash tangles in the first place during a test, and if they happen, react quickly, with no panic.

Continuing on with the test, I approach the test dog from the side while he is involved with the other dog. I will touch him and see his reaction. I will poke him gently and see if he will redirect to me; I want to see if he is locked in on the other dog or if his primary focus will come back to me.

Some dogs are so focused on other dogs that they prefer the other dogs to their handler. I want to see if I can redirect the dog back to me while he is engaged with the other dog. This is not a pass or fail aspect, but it's a bonus for a dog to prefer the company of his handler to that of the other dog. Don't get your feelings hurt if only one in a hundred dogs redirects to you. Dogs generally prefer the company of other dogs to humans.

After performing these segments – presuming all went well – I will take both dogs with me and walk around the field. I will keep them separated (one on each side of me) and walk around the field and watch their reaction. You should have adequate control of the leashes in the event they cross in front of or behind you. They should be immediately separated and you should continue the walk. It is the rarest of exceptions that will allow me to have both dogs walk on the same side. I can get a good enough indication of the dog's temperament toward each other while walking with them on either side of me.

If the test dog does fine on all aspects of these tests, there is a strong indication that he will have no issues with any dog that he will meet. It's important to note that dogs may respond differently to unfamiliar handlers. If someone is very skittish of two dogs meeting, they may trigger a response in the dog that is negative and the dog may react differently than he did in our test.

Conclusion of BARC: As a tester, it is our goal to be as fair to the dog we are testing as possible. We should understand that our evaluation is not only important to the dog we test, but also to the other dogs that this dog will encounter, as well as to the humans he will meet. We want to give every dog a fair shot at a good life and we don't want to surprise any new dog owners with a situation they are unaware or unable to control.

This test is not designed to rule out a dog from potential adoption, but rather to make educated suggestions as to the best home for a particular dog. Also, dogs that display behavioral problems during a test should be made available to animal rescue organizations so that they may rehabilitate them and place them afterwards.

I don't believe in pass or fail tests if there are rescue organizations available to take dogs that have some behavioral issues. After all, that is what rescue is supposed to be for.

By drawing some conclusions and gaining a better understanding of dogs before adopting them out, we open the doors to helping more dogs get into better homes. We also lessen the likelihood that dogs will be returned for behavioral issues. The easier we make the placement of easily adoptable dogs, the more time we can spend focused on helping the dogs that need to be rescued.

I also suggest that if people are considering adopting a dog into a home that already has a dog, they should bring their dog to meet the new candidate. This can save a lot of work, aggravation and heartache by watching their initial interaction. Introducing the dog into the home is something that should be done with time, but it is a good idea to see how two dogs will interact upon first meeting. The potential owners should be made to sign a release form to hold harmless the shelter, staff, management, etc., and the family's dog should be current on all vaccinations. If a face-to-face meeting cannot be arranged, it's a good idea to see their interaction through a gate or fence.

This is not a make-or-break introduction, but rather a basic test to see initial reactions. When introducing a new dog into a home, I suggest reading the article on www.boundangels.org entitled "Bringing Home the New Dog."

Closing thoughts: Testing a dog's behavior is a talent that is more feeling than technical. I feel that people can learn this skill to some degree, but there are those who are *naturals*. It is always best to have someone who has a natural gift to act as the tester whenever possible. This guide is designed to help people of any level to better understand canine behavior. All staff, volunteers and management who have interaction with dogs should read it, whether or not they are performing the test.

As I mentioned previously, there is an inherent risk of injury in any interaction with any dog. I strongly urge you to take caution. Caution is better than valor – and when in doubt, get **out**. Be smart about your decisions and your opinions when testing a dog. There are certain dogs that can be rehabilitated and some that cannot. I believe that those dogs that can't be helped are the smallest percentage, but they do exist. It is my goal with this book to open your eyes to better help those that can be saved, and save them.

Please download the B.A.R.C. checklist at: www.boundangels.org

Conclusion

I've dedicated thousands of hours to saving dogs. It has been the most rewarding thing I've done in my life, and in this book I hope to share this joy with you. Since this book is geared mainly to those working with difficult dogs, rescues and shelters I know that you understand the pain and torment that lives in our dogs' hearts and minds every day.

There are so many who cast aside those dogs that can't be helped by conventional ways and who leave the toughest decisions of all to someone the dog never met. Nothing can be more callous than this.

Dog training is more about patience and understanding than technique. I've seen dogs change suddenly after countless repetitions, after everyone (including me) just about gave up. Their personalities can be tough to understand, just like many people we meet. However, the extra effort that is required to understand these few has a payoff like a lottery. Seeing the transformation of a previously difficult dog into one that is a loving, obedient companion is nothing short of a miracle. This miracle is often a credit to our dedication and perseverance – nothing more.

The techniques contained in this book are a result of my work with some of the most difficult dogs that lived in the shelters I've worked with.

I've never said no to a dog that others had a problem with. I've never approached them with an "I'll show you attitude," but instead with an attitude of "Show me how you need to be understood."

Although some of the techniques in this book may seem abrupt to some, they are all proven in the best interest of the dogs that others gave up on. It's not (and never has been) my goal to make a dog do what he doesn't want to do, but rather to give him the tools he needs to live in a world controlled by man.

There are two options: live in the world according to our rules or die. Countless dogs are killed every day in our nation's shelters because of two things:

1. They can't live by the rules man imposes on them.
2. No one wants to (or is able to) help them learn to live by these rules.

I hope that by reading this book and understanding the *Difficult Dog* better, you will be better suited to helping those who cannot help themselves.

For the time and dedication you've taken upon this journey, I'm grateful. For sharing this journey with so many others, and me, I'm humbled. Please share your story with me at www.boundangels.org

Robert Cabral